Saints and Gurus

Andhra University Philosophical Studies

1. Life and Teachings of Ādi Śaṅkarācārya; by P. George Victor (ISBN 81-246-0194-1)
2. Saints and Gurus — Perspectives on Spiritual and Social Renaissance in Contemporary India; edited by P. George Victor and S.D.A. Joga Rao (ISBN 81-246-0203-4)
3. Social Relevance of Philosophy —Essays on Applied Philosophy; edited by P. George Victor (ISBN 81-246-0204-2)
4. Teaching Philosophy in the Twenty-First Century; edited by P. George Victor (ISBN 81-246-0205-0)

Andhra University Philosophical Studies, no. 2

Saints and Gurus

Perspectives on Spiritual and Social Renaissance in Contemporary India

Edited by

P. George Victor
S.D.A. Joga Rao

D.K. Printworld (P) Ltd.
New Delhi

Cataloging in Publication Data — DK

Saints and gurus: Perspectives on spiritual and social renaissance in contemporary India / edited by P. George Victor, S.D.A. Joga Rao.
(Andhra University philosophical studies; no. 2).
Includes bibliographical references.
Includes index.

1. Hindu saints — India — Congresses. 2. Gurus — India — Congresses. 3. Spiritual life — India — Congresses. I. Victor, P. George (Pasalapudi George), 1953– II. Joga Rao, S.D.A. (Srirangam Durga Ananta), 1953– III. Series: Andhra University philosophical studies; no. 2.

ISBN 81-246-0203-4

First Published in India in 2002

Published and printed by:
D.K. Printworld (P) Ltd.
Regd. office: '*Sri Kunj*', F-52, Bali Nagar
New Delhi - 110 015
Phones: (011) 545-3975; 546-6019; *Fax*: (011) 546-5926
E-mail: dkprintworld@vsnl.net

Preface

SAINTS and *guru*s have been the guiding spirit of Indian culture. Since ancient times the Indian society has been benefited by their spiritual message. Acknowledging their relevance in transcending the lot of man on earth, a national seminar on 'Living Saints and Gurus of India' was organised in the Department of Philosophy, Andhra University, Visakhapatnam on 24 and 25 August 1996 under UGC Special Assistance Programme. Scholars and spiritually inclined persons from academic institutes, seminaries, and *maṭha*s have participated in the seminar.

Inaugurating the seminar Dr. M. Gopalakrishna Reddy, the then Vice-Chancellor of Andhra University said:

> Teachings and philosophical views of saints and great philosophers turn one's life into a state of complete understanding.

He said that the ideals of Vedānta are to be inculcated in one's life for self-realisation and universal understanding that ultimately make man to realise that all religions teach the same essence to enlighten the life of man. He advised the students and scholars of philosophy to be more practical rather than theoretical.

The essays, presented at the seminar that contained in this book, attempts to bring out the metaphysical, religious, ethical and social significance of the teachings of the saints and *guru*s like Ramana Maharshi, Swami Prabhupada, Sri Chandra-sekharendra Saraswati, Mahatma Gandhi, Mother Teresa, Sri Satya Sai Baba, Sri Bala Sivayogi and, etc. They throw light on the understanding of Hindu philosophy in general, and the cultivation of a proper perspective on God, the nature of soul, spiritual equality, importance of truth and non-violence and concepts like *karma*, *jñāna* and *saṁsāra*, in particular. They also analyse the Biblical perspective on sainthood. Importantly, the book relates the significance of their thinking, addressing the imperative concerns of the present-day society and promoting universal peace and brotherhood.

The thoughts expressed in the essays reflect the testimonies of those academicians who have studied what the saints and *gurus* of India have said and practised, and also their own understanding of Indian wisdom and philosophy. The reader will have complete satisfaction out of the time he spends with this book and will get immense pleasure and a life changing experience. This book is for all those interested in Indian religion and philosophy, particularly their growth and relevance in modern context.

We are indebted to professor J.P. Shukla, Former Chairman, Indian Philosophical Congress, Professor T.S. Devadoss, UGC Nominee, Professor D.K. Chakravarty of Gauthati University, Professor B. Sambasiva Prasad of S.V. University, Dr. M.V. Ram Kumar Ratnam of Nagarjuna University for their academic encouragement.

We express our deep sense of gratitude to Dr. M. Gopalakrishna Reddy, Former Vice-Chancellor, Prof. B. Satyam, Rector, Professor G. Subrahmaniam, Former Registrar and Prof. J.M. Naidu, Registrar, Mrs. K. Samrajya Lakshmi, Finance officer of the Andhra University for their encouragement and administrative help. We are thankful to Sri Susheel K. Mittal, Director of D.K. Printworld (P) Ltd., for undertaking the publication of this work.

P. George Victor
S.D.A. Joga Rao

Contents

Introduction

Understanding Saintology

P. George Victor

VEDĀNTA is a living theology (study of God) and a religious force in India. The traditional elite, being limited with restricted human relations, imbibed the Vedāntic heritage through family and study of the scriptures while the masses imitated and inherited it through the sayings and songs of the *bhikṣu*s, *guru*s, *saṁnyāsin*s and *sādhu*s. In ordinary sense, a *bhikṣu* is a beggar for *bhikṣā* (offering), but he is a conveyor belt extraordinarily transferring the eternal truths of life to the future generations.

Like the Sophists, the wandering teachers of ancient Greece, the *bhikṣu*s, *guru*s, *saṁnyāsin*s and *sādhu*s in India have been wandering prophets. While Sophists were secular and philosophical, the *saṁnyāsin*s were ethical, religious and theological. The knowledge of the sophists was sold for a price, while the wisdom of the *bhikṣu*s, *guru*s, *saṁnyāsin*s and *sādhu*s was highly valued. The sophists were aristocratic and the *saṁnyasin*s were democratic in their method and practice. Whatever the name one chooses to call such guiding forces — *bābā*s, *bhikṣu*s, *guru*s, *muni*s, *ṛṣī*s, *sādhu*s, *svami*s, or *yogī*s they have influenced civilisation even while being out of it. They were great visionaries and missionaries with a method of comparing, comprehending and compromising with all levels of men, all states of life and with all laws of different lands. The wandering monk is a *loka kalā gama ātman*, the soul that understands the way of the world and times. This uniqueness made them popular and pragmatic. People believed them and followed them. The Sophists were for the Lords, but the *saṁnyāsin*s and *sādhu*s are for the commons.

India had a great heritage with deep-rooted culture. This was possible because of the saints, sages and monks that India had produced. Though India imports material civilisation, it is rightly exporting spiritual culture. This is due to the spirit of Vedānta that culminated in Indian minds and because of its infinite spiritual values beyond temporal reality.

Śravaṇa (listening), *manana* (remembrance) and *nididhyāsana* (meditation) were the methods adopted to teach spiritual values by great teachers of Vedānta in their ancient *āśramas* (monasteries), but the *saṁnyāsin*s and *sādhu*s lived up to them and inspired the masses. In the spiritual heritage of India, one can see great *ācārya*s (teachers of scriptures) as the advocates of *jñāna-mārga* (the path of knowledge) and critics of *karma-mārga* (the path of action) but performing *nitya* (regular), *naimittika* (occasional) and *kāmya-karma*s (desired rituals). It seems that the *saṁnyāsin*s and *sādhu*s were neither discussants on classical scriptures nor interpreters but inspiring souls.

According to Sri Bala Siva Yogendra Maharaj, there are two kinds of *guru*s: *su guru*s and *vara guru*s. *Su guru*s are the mangoes drawn from the trees in the mango garden, where as *vara guru*s are the masters divinely chosen, selected with divinebliss brought from a forest. The *vara guru*s are not traditionally trained teachers of Vedānta. Professor P.K. Mukhopadhyaya in his letter sent to the seminar director, wrote the same. For him,

> these are the persons who, even though they remained outside formal academic institutions . . . . made it possible for Vedānta to become a living faith and social force.

Richness always reflects, beauty always attracts; but when richness and beauty interlinks the stars emerge and the angels evolve reaching heights and heavens. Against the odd times of the world, against the outbreak of the star culture and against the emerging trends of materialistic tendencies, let us listen to and examine what the *saṁnyāsin*s and *sādhu*s speak about.

Philosophers have interpreted the fundamental divine concepts in various ways but the problem of the teachers of philosophy is to examine how these divine men are conducive for the good of mankind. Professor Mukhopadhyaya opines that

> the academicians and the society at large has the obligation of rescuing the profound and deep content of the teachings of these great sages and saints from the obscurantist literature produced by some overzealous devotees.

The seminar held in August 1996 was an academic exercise for unfolding the thought on saintology. In his inaugural address Sri Bala Sivayogindra Maharaj, President of Universal Peace Foundation, advised the students to take and imitate the 'Role models' for a better living, mentioning Dr. S. Radhakrishnan as a model teacher. The young Swamiji advised the students to inculcate ethical values and work for the development of the country and requested the Vice-Chancellor to introduce ethics as a subject of teaching in educational institutes. Sri Bala Sivayogi said that the society has been suffering from the division of caste and community due to mis-interpretation of the Hindu scriptures. He said:

> Today we want *Karma-yoga*. *Karma-yoga* does not mean to keep silence and to be a spectator to the happenings around us, but to strive and work to achieve the divine goal. We have great saints like Satya Sai Baba, Ramana Maharshi and Swami Jayendra Saraswathi as role models to lead a life that qualifies one to attain *mokṣa*. They are models for a life of peace and meditation.

The Swamiji referred to Mahatma Gandhi and Acarya Vinoba Bhave with reference to social life and political administration. He warned against the evil practices in the society and advised the people not to be carried away by them. He said that every man is potentially a saint, if one realises and practises the divine way to the Almighty.

Reverend Dr. P.J. Titus, Founder and President of the C.O.T.R. College of Ministries, Bhimili, spoke on 'Biblical and Christian Perspective on Saints and Sages'. Dr. P.J. Titus said that Gandhiji's teachings have international application.

> Every Christian is a saint. Sainthood is a divine imperative; it is the character and nature of God. The Love of God includes every human being; sainthood is a call, a great commission to go and make disciples.

It is surprising to note that both Sri Bala Sivayogi, the Hindu religious leader and Rev. Dr. P.J. Titus, the Christian missionary have asserted that every person is potentially a saint. The Swāmījī also explained that every individual was potentially a saint, and that whosoever thought on God was a Swamiji meditating upon God. Worshipping a saint as a divine God and ultimately as God, depends upon the attitude and thinking of each individual with reference to his tradition and education. Whatever be the scriptures, they are there to assert the oneness of human beings and not to discriminate among them. According to these men of two different religions, the society does not need theoretical explanations but a helping hand to the people at grassroot level. The meaning of the *tat tvam asi,* the doctrine of the Upaniṣads and Saint Paul's assertion that 'Man is the temple of God' in the *Bible* have the same spiritual message.

1

Sri Vijnananidhitirtha Swamiji

Universal Understanding

V. Badarayana Murthy

THE organisers of the seminar invited papers on the living saints, sages and *guru*s of India who have worked in their own way for the unity of the country and also upheld the Vedāntic tradition. This reminds me of a real sage-saint-*guru* who was with us till quite recently, but is now no more. Yet, for me and for a few others he is a living saint as he haunts our minds and often plays our roles even now. He is Sri Dayanidhitirtha Swamiji, who had occupied the Seat of Pontiff of Sri Sripadaraja Maṭha, Mulbagal, in the Kolar district. His outstanding qualification can be gleaned from the following verse:

mauna lakṣaṇa sampūrṇam jñāna sampat su vaibhavam ।
dayānidhi gurum vande tattva mārga sudarśakam ।।

One of his disciples is Sri Vijnananidhitirtha Swamiji, the present pontiff of Sri Sripadaraja Maṭha, the sponsor of which was Sri Padmanabhatirtha Swami, the very first disciple of Sri Madhvacarya. Sri Vijnananidhitirtha Swamiji generally stays in Bangalore but often goes on tours. I would consider him as a sage-saint-*guru* for all practical purposes.

The one sagely quality in him is that he knows his limitations and aspires to rise higher. Like Socrates, he declares, 'I know that I don't know'. Nevertheless, he is certainly a sage who highly reveres Sri Dayanidhitirtha Swamiji and remembers the wise sayings uttered by the saintly master often in the form of English proverbs:

Eat to live, not live to eat;
Don't trouble troubles unless troubles trouble you;
Tell me your company and I will tell you what you are;
Adapt or Perish.

Before becoming pontiff as Sri Vijnananidhitirtha Swami, Sri H.K. Bhimasenacharya, with good schooling up to P.U.C., was very good at science and mathematics. As president of Mulbagal Municipality, he was bold and honest. The local Citizens and even high official dignitaries found him to be a challenge. Personally, he led an austere spiritual life. Hunger never stood in the way of his official as well as spiritual duties. In the evenings, he regularly attended lessons on sacred texts conducted by an eminent scholar — Sri Hayagrivacharya.

After assuming charge as pontiff of the Maṭha, with the holy name of Sri Vijnananidhitirtha, his personal qualities have taken thoroughly a new turn, quite fitting his new status. He, who was a noble terror as municipal president, has now become quite adaptable to circumstances and maintains a peaceful atmosphere in the affairs of the Maṭha. Though wrongs done by others rouse his ire, he settles the affairs somehow and keeps calm. His daily routine is noteworthy. After morning ablution, he goes through the necessary spiritual observances and then sits repeating the *OṀKĀRA mantra* 3000 times with due concentration. Whenever there is a break between spiritual duties and obligations and brief periods of rest, he continuously goes on reading useful literature of all kinds.

Swamiji is not a *paṇḍit* in the usual sense, but his *janmāntara saṁskāra* and his reverence to the spiritual master Sri Dayanidhitirtha Swami have made him a questioner like Socrates. He wants good analogies from life to substantiate one's statements. He insists on scientific data wherever possible to clarify concepts. For example, he asks how transcendence from the physical to the spiritual actually takes place. Many are at a loss to answer the question squarely. *Paṇḍit*s are generally ignorant of modern science and scientists are strangers to spirituality. The mode of getting the answer is by asking the scientist what is that 'he' which speaks as 'my mind, my brain'. The next question would be — 'why are you sometimes good and sometimes not so good or even bad?' The ultimate question would be about the immanence of the omniscient, omnipotent Supreme Being who prompts the embodied self and bridges the material and the spiritual.

Another question the Swamiji poses is 'How can the Supreme Being, who is in His fullness both in the mega and the mini, be considered as a part of the whole (*aṁśa*)'. I said that the concept of *aṁśa* is with reference to his manifestation in the material world, which consists of parts and wholes. It is like the self, like the same electric current showing lesser or greater brilliance in bulbs of different capacities. He agreed and supplemented my answer by saying that the Supreme Being is not an inactive mass of self-knowledge; he is omnipotent. Although there is no difference whatsoever between Himself and His *satchidānanda svarūpa*, they being different aspects of one and the same personality, His abilities are such that He can accommodate Himself to the needs of different things and beings. Śrī Mādhvācārya considers this accommodative ability as the *viśeṣa lakṣaṇa* of the Supreme Being. The Swamiji brings in the analogy of the pinhole camera to explain how the mega can become the mini and the vice versa.

Swamiji is of the opinion that the emergence of the Advaita, Viśiṣṭādvaita and Dvaita Schools of interpretation is a natural development in the historical sense. It is thus that the Lord purposely deluded the undeserving demoniac souls by dwelling upon the harmful nature of Vedic sacrifices. But while the wise ones just abstained from animal sacrifices, the extremists among Buddhists preached against the veracity of the Vedas and proclaimed '*Śūnyavāda*' or blank peaceful end. Śrī Śaṅkarācārya lifted up the Vedas to their prestigious heights and highlighted the presence of an eternal self, without whom the existence in the world would be meaningless. Śrī Mādhvācārya has praised the Buddha as

> *daitya vamohaka niṭya-sukhade deva subodhaka buddha svarūpa,*
> *ditisutamohana vimala subhodana paraguṇa buddha he bhava mama śaraṇam.*

Recognising the miserable course of life here on the earth, Śrī Ramanujācārya distinguished between the suffering soul and the ever-joyful Supreme Soul and laid stress on the need for devotional self-surrender. But he did not clearly state the relationship between the souls and the Supreme Soul. Some of his statements like *ānanda sāmya* were stretched beyond their logical limits by the followers. Therefore, Sri Madhvacarya had to clarify the Vedāntic concept still further saying:

(i) The individual souls and the Supreme Being are quite distinct, not one and the same and different as well. Being different does not mean having separate existence outside the Universal Self. It means that the Supreme Being is both within and without everything and every being, and things and being find their existence in Him.

(ii) The Universe is not the body of the Supreme Self, but He treats it as if it were His body in order to motivate the embodied souls through the physical media.

(iii) There is similarity between the joy of the realised souls and the joy of the Supreme Self, merely so far as the connotation of the word goes. This is *ānanda sāmya*. But the *ānanda* of the Lord is incomparable, both qualitatively and quantitatively.

Sri Vijnananidhitirtha Swamiji has a broad outlook like his spiritual master and gives due respect to everyone, irrespective of caste or creed. In fact, one may be surprised to learn that the spiritual master, Sri Dayanidhitirtha Swamiji treated a Muslim boy — Abdul Lateef, with kind hospitality, and that the boy grew up with my children while he was a High School student. The master was adept in recognising the intrinsic worth of souls behind the body marks.

We, Sri Vijanananidhitirtha Swamiji and myself, give due respect to all religious faiths, knowing full well that they are all off-shoots of the same Vedāntic origin, as can be seen from reverence given to *oṁ, amen* and *ameen* respectively by Vedāntins, Christians and Muslims. They are only different trends in the historical course of the universe.

Sri Vijnananidhitirtha Swamiji seems to have acquired high efficiency by virtue of his spiritual routine. The Swamiji blessed a girl, who was quite indifferent about her success in a proficiency examination, and she obtained a high first class. Now, she is leading a happy married life. A decrepit patient, who was so disabled that he could not move his limbs freely and had to lie helplessly, and who did not get relief by long medical treatment, was blessed by the Swami's touch and he is now able to move about freely. But, the Swamiji is not a miracle-monger at that. Very few people know of such *tapa siddhi* attained by him.

At a large gathering in Chennai (Madras), where the elite had assembled to honour him, the Swamiji spoke about the Dvaita view of Vedānta in such a way that they were spellbound, as it were. He dwelt upon the historical aspect of the rise of monism, monistic dualism and dualism, one following the other, to meet the needs of the times when they were propounded. As usual, he resorted to a scientific analogy — that of the molecular, atomic and the quantum theories emerging in succession. For those who had been overpowered by the *Śūnyavāda* of the later Buddhists, highlighting the veracity of the Vedic dictum and pinpointing the presence of *ātman* was more than enough and that was achieved by Śrī Śaṅkarācārya. Śrī Rāmānujācārya preached the inseparable existence of individual souls and the need for devotional surrender. Śrī Madhvācārya went further and classified the individual souls into three categories — those that are eligible for salvation, those that are designated for eternal damnation and those that reach an eternal state of mixed happiness. The Swamiji pointed out that it was quite in conformity with the verdict of the 16th to 18th chapters of the *Bhagavad Gītā*. He clarified the relationship between the ever-independent, the Supreme Being and the ever-dependent, individual souls by bringing in the analogy of the sensory organ, eye. The eye has the ability to see. But, in a dark room, it cannot see. However, with the aid of external light, its ability is roused.

When the Swamiji related this episode, I intervened and said that the bridging of Dvaita and Advaita lies in using the same analogy in a more meaningful manner. The eye has to be motivated by external light; but the individual soul is motivated by the Supreme Being, who is both within and without, everywhere. He is the Soul of all Souls. They act only when He acts their roles. "He thinks our thoughts, does our deeds, reaps our crops, but makes us eat the fruits thereof". So much so, there is perfect identity between the Actor self and the Individual Self. This, I believe, is the import of the great sentence *tat tvam asi*. But, although the Supreme Being can act the role of the individual soul, the latter can never act the role of the former, even after release. The analogy of the river waters becoming one with the seawater fits well with the Advaita view of oneness.

The Swamiji was glad and supplemented my viewpoint, saying that Śrī Mādhvācārya had proclaimed the same thing, *advaitaḥ paramārthataḥ*. In conclusion, I wish to say that Sri Vijnananidhitirtha Swamiji is a living sage-saint-*guru* for all practical purposes, so far as I know.

2

Satya Sai Baba: A Prophet of God

V. Badarayana Murthy

THIS article deals with the interpretation of Vedānta in general and with the saintly role played by Sri Satya Sai Baba in particular.

Vedānta or Upaniṣad is specifically meant for special instruction to an ardent disciple who is eager to learn *ātma vidyā*, the mode of self-realisation. If prevailing social evils are to be eradicated to a considerable extent to make people happy and progressive like true human beings, they should be made to give due regard to metaphysical, ethical, religious and civic values.

The major religions of the world — Hinduism, Christianity and Islam — are unanimous in their reverence to the Word of God. The metaphysical and ethical values of religions made people happy in spite of natural calamities and wars. But now, with all the gadgets meant for providing happiness, people are not really happy. Greed and selfishness of individuals and nations are the root causes for such a sorry state of affairs. The remedy lies in reviving respect for religion and religious practices, at least to a minimum extent in the latter case. Mere adoration of modern science and rationalism and educational equipment just for material benefits leads nowhere near peace and true happiness.

The responsibility of improving the tone of the social structure lies in the hands of saints, sages, and *gurus*. No single person can shoulder this responsibility unless he is a chosen prophet of God. Therefore, the well-intentioned saints must form religious organisations for social welfare. But the trouble in the formation of such organisations is that even enlightened saints have no consensus with regard to the interpretation of Vedānta. Not that there cannot be consensus; but prejudices and loyalties come in its way.

Prabhupada and Ramana Maharshi were indeed prophets chosen by God — one, a loud gatherer and the other, the most silent *guru*. The ISKCON (International Society for Krishna Consciousness) is a spectacular example of the achievement of a modern prophet. My personal contact with ISKCON tells that, except for a few stray cases, most of the followers — both foreign and Indian — are sincere and happy. Similarly, those who are associated with the Ramakrishna Mission and Ramana Maharshi Ashramas are also breathing peace.

Another saint who is right now amongst us and is wielding wide useful influence is Satya Sai Baba. Although I am not a subscriber to the Sai Cult, I have admiration for the personality of Sri Satya Sai Baba and his achievements.

Unlike Dr. H. Narasimhiah, Dr. Cavour and the host of non-believers in miracles I know how miracles are brought about by simple faith, by invoking spirits and by yogic culture. For instance, in Mulbagal of Kolar district, every year a *jātrā* of Mariyamma takes place, when even innocent ladies with articles of worship on their heads, walk upon burnt logs of fire over a distance of about 10-12 ft sustaining no injury. That is a matter of pure faith. They don't need scientific tricks like Dr. Cavour. Dr. Narasimhiah's devotion to science is laudable, but his approach to test the genuineness of miracles is wrong. One cannot say, 'God, if you really exist, come and stand before me'. God is not so cheap, nor is Sri Satya Sai Baba.

To know the truth about the higher sort of miracles, one should know how real the yogic practice is. It is not merely performing a few *yogāsana*s and breathing exercises and simple meditation to achieve a kind of blank calmness. The first five parts of yogic practice — *yama*, *niyama*, *āsana*, *prāṇāyāma* and *pratyāhāra* — are meant to achieve mind control. The next three steps — *dhyāna*, *dhāraṇā* and *samādhi* — are prescribed to help form and retain a mental picture of the desired deity with full concentration. When the last step is perfected, the deity will condescend to bless the *yogī* with supernatural powers (*aṣṭa siddhi*s): *animā*, *mahimā*, *garimā*, *laghimā*, *prāpti*, *prakāmya*, *īśatva* and *vasitva* (growing smaller or bigger, heavier or lighter, achievement, fulfilling wishes, mastery and subjugation). What has been well achieved in previous births may stand in good stead in the future periods of life too. The case of Sri Satya Sai Baba seems to be one of previous achievements.

This, being the case, how can rationalists understand the efficacy of *yantra*, *tantra* and *mantra*. They are *nāstika*s who can never be convinced. Unless they become *āstika*s, their doom is sealed.

The Baba himself has said that he is the same as Shirdi Sai Baba and that he is going to be born again in Karnataka, Mandya district to complete his mission. His achievement as the saint of Shirdi is most noteworthy. Many of his devotees are religious-minded and god-fearing persons of noble culture. The achievements of Sri Satya Sai Baba, too, are quite stupendous as can be judged by the number of highly intelligent devotees and the Sai institutions that have sprung up. He gets funds of unimaginable proportions, but all that is used for social good.

If one goes round Prasantinilayam at Puttaparti, it can be seen how Vedānta has been interpreted in an all-embracing practical form taking into its fold people of all communities and religions. The huge statues of Hanumān, Śīva, Jesus and Prophet Muhammad tell us about the breadth of Vedāntic vision, which declares *sarvam khalvidam brahma*. The hospital at 'Prasantinilayam' is as miraculous as the saint himself, providing free treatment for the most complicated cases.

Satya Sai Baba is great and has human traits, which one should take into consideration. The body may display *sāttvika* or *rājasika* or *tāmasika* or mixed traits according to *prārabdha karma śeṣa*, but the soul can remain unaffected if *sādhanā* is ripe. I know there will be many who take me to task either for winking at weaknesses or for talking so lightly about the saint who is considered as *Bhagavān*. Although, personally, I do not consider Sri Baba as 'God Himself', I can daresay that he is chosen by God to do a great job, viz., turning people's minds towards God and religion.

Highly learned and discreet persons approach Baba for blessings, for example, former President of India Sri Shankar Dayal Sharma and former Chief Election Commissioner Sri T.N. Seshan. They are not gullible boors and not 'junglees'. Many approach Baba humbly because he can scan their plights and provide solutions for their problems. Of course, some unscrupulous magnates may also approach him with huge presents. But it is like guilty persons depositing lakh of rupees in Lord Venkaṭeśvara's *huṇḍi*. They too are blessed for their faith, but not fully in proportion to the deposit; and the Lord knows how to distribute the offerings.

Sri Baba has the ability to scan others' minds. Once, when he was in Bangalore at the National High School premises long back, a teacher of that High School, Sri H.S. Srinivasa Murthy, a friend of mine and a Madhva like myself, was lingering in the crowd reluctantly with his own apprehensions about the personality of Baba. Srinivasa Murthy was mentally repeating a verse praising the guardianship of Sri Vayudeva. The saint beckoned to him and as the teacher approached hesitantly, said in Telugu, "You are reciting the verse *Matarme matariswan*; You may go; You have no place here".

I have not seen Baba personally, but I have had a great deal of first-hand information from one of my assistant masters, Sri S. Vasudeva Rao, whose father Sri Venkataramaiah was worshipper at Prasantinilayam. Vasudeva Rao and his wife used to visit Puttaparti three to four times every year on special occasions and they would tell me about their experiences. Once, it seems, Vasudeva Rao's wife had lost her *māṅgalyam* that had slipped from her neck. She searched everywhere in vain and ran up to Baba in great distress. The saint told her that she could find the *māṅgalyam* behind the door of the room that they had occupied. It was exactly so. I was told that when marriages were celebrated at Prasantinilayam, Baba would bring out *sārīs* and *dhotīs*, just by waving his hand, to present them to the bride and the bridegroom as also to their parents. It was not a matter of producing small gift articles or ashes by sleight of hand as even Dr. Cavour could do.

Sri Sai Baba is not a self-styled godman. Those who saw God in him revered him by calling him *Bhagavān*. I am told that even as a boy of sixteen, with no intention of cheating, he went and stood behind the *Śivaliṅga* at Hampī to signify that Lord Śiva was in him. I am also told that once he walked into the sea a long way and disappeared. Those, whom he had left on the shore, were highly alarmed; but, to their surprise, they saw the image of Lord Anantha Padmanabha instead. Then, Baba appeared again with them. In this respect, he was like Sri Ramakrishna Paramahamsa who displayed the figure of Śrī Rāma within his body.

For those who are familiar with Vedānta, this phenomenon is not a mystery in the usual sense. The Supreme Being is the Soul of every other Soul. He acts the roles of other souls for their sake as they solely depend on Him: *dravyam karma ca kalaśca svabhāvo jīva eva ca; yad anugrahataḥ santi na santi yad upekṣayā*. When an embodied soul has reached a particular level of *sādhanā*, God in him may show Himself as He is to devotee onlookers. The physical body of everyone really belongs to the Supreme Being and belongs to the Soul by way of 'Reflection' (*pratibimba-bhāva*) through the medium of 'Ego'.

Hindus now have lost touch with the significance of *mantra*s recited at the time of wedding. The girl's father says, *imam lakṣmi kanyām lakṣmī nārāyaṇa varaya dāsye*. It means that the wedding is primarily between Lakṣmī Devī and Śrīmān Nārāyaṇa on behalf of the girl and the boy. An important fact to remember in this affair is that Śrīman Nārāyaṇa is in Lakṣmī Devī like herself and the wedding is between his male role and his female role, just to make Lakṣmī Devī joyful and to bless the wedded couple. The Supreme Being is neither male, nor female, nor neuter. Sri Ramakrishna Paramahamsa worshipped Lord Śrī Rāma like a Hindu, worshipped Jesus like a Christian and Prophet Muhammad like a Muslim. Sri Sai Baba too gives due respect to every form of God as can be seen by the huge statues installed at Prasantinilayam.

Before concluding this article I wish to point out that although things seem to be going from bad to worse day-by-day, it is indeed the 'golden age' for those who understand the message of Vedānta. Half-baked *paṇḍit*s may distract us. Hoaxes may betray us. Yet, if we learn the message of Vedānta by right interpretation, we can sail smooth without the rigours of the earlier ages like *tapas*, 'sacrifices' and elaborate worship. Every religion, every shade of philosophy, has its own scheme to shape the destiny of the trainee soul, life after life. All seasons make a year and all religions season a soul for self-realisation. Though it may be out of place, I am tempted to say how I often dream of having been born as a Christian in England in one of my previous births.

What is required, therefore, is mutual understanding and friendly respect for each other. But that does not mean that we should synthesise the philosophies and religious practices of others into ours and make a mess of things like Akbar who formulated *Dīn-ī-ilāhī* and failed. The very message of Vedānta is to perceive the scheme of the Omniscient Lord in everything that has been brought into creation and also His omnipresence as *jagannāṭaka sūtradhārī*. If this *samadarśī-tattva* is apprehended and practised by more and more numbers of the wise, the better it would be for the welfare of the society. May God bless us with better understanding and better social relationships. May the right interpretations of Vedānta prevail.

3

Ramana Maharshi: His Philosophy

B.V.S. Bhanusree

RAMANA Maharshi was born in 1879 in a village of Tirhchuzhi near Madurai in Tamil Nadu. As a schoolboy he was intelligent and active. But at the age of seventeen, suddenly he had a strange and wonderful experience. He was sitting alone in his room when a sudden and inexplicable fear of death took hold of him. He became acutely aware that he was going to die, although outwardly he was in good health. The thing was a psychological phenomenon, because there was no apparent reason why he should die. Yet he became obsessed with this notion and immediately began to prepare for the coming event.

He stretched his body upon the floor, fixed his limbs with the rigidity of a corpse, closed his eyes and mouth and finally held his breath. To say in his own words:

> Well then, this body is dead. It will be carried stiff to the burning ground and then reduced to ashes. But with the death of the body, am I dead? Is the body I? This body is now silent stiff. But I continue to feel the full force of my Self apart from its condition.[1]

It is a rare incident that occurred to him with no quest, no striving, no conscious preparation. Normally some study is needed, followed by long and arduous training, often lasting a whole lifetime but more often still incomplete at the end of a lifetime. As the sages say, it depends on the spiritual maturity of a person.

Ramana emerged from this amazing experience an utterly changed youth. Paul Brunton explained

> He lost most of his interest in studies, sports, friends and so on because his chief interest was now centred in the sublime consciousness of the true self, which he had found so unexpectedly. Fear of death vanished as mysteriously as it came. He enjoyed an inward serenity and spiritual strength which have never since left him. . . .
>
> He gave up old habits and tried to be alone as much as possible, for then he would sink into meditation and surrender himself to the absorbing current of divine consciousness, which constantly drew his attention inwards.[2]

But his family members resented this sudden change in him. Their attitude provoked him to leave home and lead the life of *sādhu* at Tiruvannamalai. He lived there for more than fifty years teaching the path of self-enquiry to all, who came from India and abroad, from East and West. An *āśrama* grew up around him. He had become *maharṣi*, Great Sage, a title traditionally given to one who preaches a new spiritual path. Though he was not interested in any sort of worldly life, he was forced to live for the devotees and breathed his last in 1950, at around the age of seventy-one.

Ramana Maharshi did not propound any new theory. What he taught was the ultimate doctrine of non-duality or Advaita in which all other doctrines are finally absorbed. That Being is one and is manifested in the universe and in all creatures without ever changing from its eternal, unmanifest Self. Much as, in a dream, the mind creates all the people and events a man sees without losing anything by their creation or gaining anything by their re-absorption, without ceasing to be itself. He taught all in a dialogue form. He never encouraged the questions that were asked for mere gratification of curiosity. But he had enormous patience to explain when questions bore upon the task of self-discovery. Mainly, he taught through the tremendous power of spiritual silence.

The method of enquiry into oneself that he taught goes beyond philosophy and beyond psychology, for it is not the qualities of the ego that are sought but the self-standing resplendent without qualities. What the mind has to do is not to suggest a reply, but to remain quiet so that the true reply can arise. If you keep on asking, by concentrating on the spiritual centre the reply will come.

Self-enquiry

The Self is self-effulgent, which transcends darkness and light. One should not think of it with the mind. The Self is the pure Reality, in whose light the body, the ego and all else shine. The ego springs from ignorance; it confuses and misleads a man to think of self in the form of body, mind, etc. . . . Maharshi suggested *bhakti* (devotion), *jñāna* (knowledge), *yoga* (union), or *dhyāna* (meditation) to root out the *māyā* (illusion). Maharshi explains that the mind and the ego are one and the same. Intellect, will, ego and individuality are collectively the same mind. It is like a man being variously described according to his different activities. The individual is nothing else than the ego which, again, is only the mind. Simultaneously with the rise of the ego the mind appears, associated with the reflected nature of the Self, like the red-hot iron in the example.[3] The red-hot iron is the individual, the fiery heat is the witnessing Self, the iron is the ego. The pure fire is the all-immanent and all-knowing Supreme Spirit.

Waking, dream and sleep are mere phases of the mind, not of the Self. The Self is the witness of these three states. Our true nature exists in sleep. Though present even in sleep, the Self is not then perceived. It cannot be known in sleep straight away. It must first be realised in the waking state for it is our true nature underlying all the three states. Effort must be made in the waking state and the Self realised here and now. It will then be understood to be the continuous self, uninterrupted by the alternation of waking, dream and deep-sleep. In the fourth state, the ego merges in consciousness; as in sleep it does in unconsciousness.

Maharshi explains that heart is the true seat of consciousness; but by this he did not mean the physical organ at the left side of the chest, but the 'spiritual heart' at the right, and by 'consciousness' he did not mean thought but pure awareness or sense of being. He had found it from his own experience to be the centre of spiritual awareness and then found his experience confirmed in some ancient texts.[4]

Maharshi's technique of self-enquiry is something different from meditation. He explains that meditation is more or less mental, but the quest for the Self is a direct method and is superior to it.

> For the moment you get into the quest for the Self and begin to go deeper. The real self is waiting there to receive you, and then whatever is to be done is done by something else and you as an individual have no hand in it. In this process all doubts and discussions are automatically given up, just as one who sleeps forgets all his cares for the time being.[5]

In order to end both the world and its miseries, *Bhagavān* suggests to turn inwards and seek the self. He says that the world and its sufferings are unreal. Pain is nothing but a feeling for him. As long as one thinks that the body or the objective world is real there exists suffering. But once he realises the Self there is no more pain as the Self is Reality, Absolute and beyond all the suffering.

The path of self-enquiry of Maharshi is a new integrated one which embraces *karma-mārga* (path of action) and *jñāna-mārga* (path of knowledge). The ancient path of self-enquiry was pure *jñāna-mārga* to be followed in silent meditation by the hermit and had, moreover, been considered by the sages as unsuited to this *kaliyuga*, this spiritually dark age in which we live. What *Bhagavān* did was

> not so much to restore the old path as to create a new one adapted to the conditions of our age, a path that can be followed in city or household no less than in forest or

> hermitage, with a period of meditation each day and constant remembering throughout the day's activities, with or without the support of outer observances.[6]

When asked about the four *āśramas*, Maharshi replied that it was a social rule intended for the majority. But

> if one is a *Pakvi*, a well-developed being, he need not mind this rule. Young or old, man or woman, Brahmin or outcast, if one is *Pari-pakvi*, fully ripe, he or she can and does go straight to the goal, without minding the stages.

When the *brahmacārin*, with his purity exalted by celibacy, becomes by detachment an ideal householder for the service of others, or of society, the height naturally flashes forth. Then for the purpose of *tapas*, for concentrated effort, the third *āśrama*, *vānaprastha* is intended. When by ardent *tapas*, the *tapasvin* becomes crystal-pure and fit, the fourth *āśrama* automatically comes. *Saṁnyāsa* does not lie in taking to the begging bowl, or having a clean bald-headed shave, or putting on an orange-coloured robe.

To conclude, Ramana Maharshi's philosophy is more practical. He realised that mere book learning is not of any great use. After Realisation all intellectual loads are useless burdens and are to be thrown overboard. That's why he suggested turning our minds inward and being happy in realising the Self. He also suggested not to go for the things beyond but to concentrate on the present problem. Though he was deeply involved in self-enquiry, for the sake of the people he came out and taught the Reality.

Reference

1. Quoted from Arthur Osborne, *The Collected Works of Ramana Maharshi*, 1959, p. viii.
2. Paul Brunton, *The Maharshi and His Message*, 1994, p. 54.

*The mind, which is made up of thoughts, arises out of consciousness.

The essence of the mind is only awareness or consciousness. However, when the ego overclouds it, it functions as reasoning, thinking or perceiving. The universal mind, not being, not being limited by the ego, has nothing outside itself and is therefore only aware. The ego-ridden mind has its strength sapped and is too weak to resist distressing thoughts. The egoless mind is happy, as we see in deep, dreamless sleep. Clearly, therefore, happiness and distress are only modes of the mind. *Vide*: Arthur Osborne, *The Teachings of Bhagavan Sri Ramana Maharshi in His Own Words*, pp. 21-2.

3. It is a commonly used example in India that just as red-hot iron partakes of the nature of the fire through contact with it, so the mind or ego partakes of the nature of consciousness through contact with the self. *Vide*: Arthur Osborne, *Collected Works of Ramana Maharshi*, p.13.

4. A Malayali book on *Ayurveda and in the Sita Upaniṣad*, Talks with Sri Ramana Maharshi, *ibid.*, p. 4.

5. Arthur Osborne, *The Teachings of Bhagavan Sri Ramana Maharshi in His Own Words*, pp. 19-20.

6. Arthur Osborne, *The Collected Works of Ramana Maharshi*, p. xv.

4

Sri Satya Sai Baba's Approach to Vedānta

V. Gopalakrishnaiah

Bhagavan Sri Satya Sai Baba lives in Prasantinilayam, Puttaparti, Andhra Pradesh. He is a Baba who has dedicated his life for spreading divine ideas, which he has discovered. His works are being read throughout the world. In preparing a paper on Satya Sai Baba, I have depended on his work entitled *Conversations with Bhagavan Sri Satya Sai Baba*.

Miracles

Sri Satya Sai Baba is a great person for his followers. He, on several occasions, has produced from his hands sugar candy, *vibhūdhi*, gold rings, ear rings, *Śīva-liṅga*s and photos for his devotees. He is a remarkable person and he introduced *Sat Saṅgha* for the suffering folk. Moreover he has healing capacity for the diseased people. Bhagavan Sri Satya Sai Baba has devotees not only in India but also in countries like the USA. Foreign visitors come to him and have *darśana* of him.

His ideas

When time, work, reason and experience are in harmony, they constitute truth. When the four are found to be not in harmony, then it is untruth. Full light is wisdom and full dark is ignorance. The cure for this disease of ignorance is *sādhanā*. Truth is one and for all time, truth is truth. Life is truth and that is God. The unchangeable is truth.

Satya Sai Baba tells first 'I', then 'You', that is the work. 'I' plus 'You' is 'We'. 'We' plus 'He' is God. One must have physical strength, spiritual strength and mental strength. Then only one can do some service. In his view love is God; one has to live in love: love itself is God. There are different forms of love like love for family and love for money; but love for God is devotion. In India rice and wheat are standard. They are all right if taken in moderation. But people eat too much and get dull. Too much food results in dullness of mind; food in moderation does not result in sickness. Swami travels to various parts of India and does not get sick from eating.

Anything that comes from the cow, a little milk, butter, cheese, is all right for the spiritual aspirant. Satya Sai Baba is *kalpataru* tree. He gives anything to his devotees. According to Baba, the body comes and goes but the *ātmā* is permanent. The body has birth and death. The spirit does not have any of these. Speaking on meditation, Satya Sai Baba tells that in meditation one gets sense control. *Yoga* helps one with the body. And when mind is steady, concentration will come automatically. When one gets such concentration, then one gets peace of mind. Faith is the foundation and surrender is the peak.

One sees a plane in the sky. He cannot see the pilot; to see the pilot, he must buy a ticket. The Universe also has a Pilot. He is God. To see Him the ticket is his grace. Swami tells that money comes to one's hands, but does not stay. Whereas morality comes and stays, money comes and goes; morality comes and grows. On *mantra*s he tells as follows. The experts in *mantra*s were called saints. The experts in machines are called scientists. The Vedas come from certain fundamental sounds and their variations. The scientific modification of the sound changes the meaning of what is said. No written language is able to represent all of the Vedic sounds. It is impossible to write many of the words. The Vedas are God's breath and can be transmitted from person to person by voice.

Baba's *avatāra* has taken body to revive *dharma*. He is here, engaged in that. The central part of Swami's teaching in regard to living in the world is to see in other people that essential quality which is God and to love that quality and not be bothered by all the actions, qualities, misbehaviour, characteristics of the persons. According to him, intelligence, which is discrimination, is not the mind, nor is it the thought; Intelligence is direct *ātma-śakti*. He says that day-by-day one's life is shortened and one surrenders to time, and time is God. Time conquers one's life and that time is God. In the same way, all is God. Thoughts, desires, all are God. All thoughts should be regarded as God.

Vedānta

Satya Sai Baba tells that Vedānta is metaphysical inquiry of the divine, the world, and the valid experience of each. Metaphysics begins where physics ends. Vedānta proves by experience that which has been formulated. Philosophy is the fruit that has all the parts, whereas Vedānta is the sweet juice. Philosophy takes you to the edge of truth, gives you the vision of truth; Vedānta takes you to the heart of truth. Philosophy is a way of intellectual inquiry. Swami is the activator of the individual. He is the 'I' in you and in everyone, as it is said in Advaita.

According to Sai Baba, one should have a mental image of a form of God, fully developed, the mind poured into that form. When the image of God is seen outside, it is qualified dualism. When seen in the mind it is qualified monism. When the form is absorbed into the *ātmā*, that is, Advaita, non-dualism. The two preliminary steps are not separate stages; they are contained in Advaita, as buttermilk and butter are contained in milk. The image of God seen outside should be taken into the mind and then into the soul. Baba delved into the thought of Indian sages and saints. In the opinion of his followers he is the globe and the universe.

Liberation

Baba tells that one must tackle this problem from where it starts. Ignorance can be cured only by knowledge, darkness can be destroyed only by light. No amount of argument or threat or persuasion can compel darkness to move away; a flash of light is enough and darkness is gone. One has to prepare for that flash of illumination; the light is in him. But, since it is heavily overridden by repressing factors, it cannot reveal itself. The liberation comes when the light is revealed; this is called *mokṣa*. Everyone has to achieve it. Whether he is striving for it now or not. It is the inevitable end to the struggle, the goal towards which all are proceeding.

How should one prepare oneself for that stage? Baba tells that the word *mokṣa* contains the answer. It is self-explanatory. *Mo* indicates *moha* (delusion) — being deluded by the scintillating, the gaudy, the transitory, the temporary trash; and *kṣa* means *kṣaya* (decline) — disappearance, destruction. One has to keep the flights of his mind away from these deluding attractions and on the straight path to liberation. According to Bhagavan Sri Satya Sai Baba, one can get *mokṣa* by faith, *japa* and *bhakti* in reciting the names of God such as Jesus, Rāma and Kr̥ṣṇa. Sai Baba is an excellent sage and saint and god of contemporary times.

5

Swami Bala Siva Yogi and I

M. Gopalakrishna Reddy

In Delhi, sometime in March 1975, when I was reading *The Holy Science* of Swami Yukteswar, a co-guest in the guest-house where I stayed, V. Kuppuswamy, Assistant Director of Treasuries and Accounts, Government of Andhra Pradesh, seeing my interest in spiritual matters told me of Swami Bala Siva. He had had several experiences with Him. He narrated a few of them and suggested that I should have Swami's *darśana* (gracious presence/ look).

It was months later in October 1975 that Swami came to Vishakhapatnam with Bhattam Sriramamurthy, then Minister in the Government of Andhra Pradesh. As soon as I heard of Him, I rushed to the Circuit House where He was staying. Strangely, I did not go there alone but along with my wife, which I normally never did. When we had *darśana* he was squatting on the floor in *padmāsana* (lotus pose), one or two others were there, including an old friend of mine Venkatarao of the Central Excise Department. We did prostrations to Swami. He gave us *vibhūti* (sacred ash), which he materialised at will, and also a *rudrākṣa* to me. I was then reading Sai Baba's miracles and yearning to see him. Swami said, as though he had read my mind, that I could do this magic just as my Sai Baba.

Towards the end of December, the same year, Swami was in Vizag (Vishakhapatnam) again. He stayed with Parasuram Patrudu, an Advocate friend of mine. Swami gave a discourse at Vivekananda Hall. A large gathering of devotees who had come there heard it spellbound. I was asked to chant *oṁ namaḥ śivāya* and lead the chorus. Returning from the meeting hall, Swami said to me in the car that I was yearning to see the light beyond and that he would show it to me. Yes, I was yearning to see the light from the time I had read Yogānanda's autobiography and received Swami Hariharananda's blessings. I wondered, "How did he know it?" I immediately jumped at the idea. Some lurking fear however was there in the mind as to what this experience would be like. Swami materialised a *sindūra* box made of silver with a wave of his hand, put *tilaka* on my forehead, presented me with the box and took me to the next room. Asking me to close my eyes in the dark, he showed me that light, that conscious sea of light, thousandfold brighter than the sun. I felt that I had first passed through the blue sky. I saw the planets, the stars pass by and the whole universe was before me. In the waves of brilliant white light that started thereafter profound peace was felt. It may be the same *darśana* called *viśvarūpa darśana* that was shown to Arjuna by Lord Kṛṣṇa for giving to Arjuna the realisation 'Thou art That'. It was all over in less than two minutes. But strange calm and peace settled in me for several days.

I was in Hyderabad in the following March to have *darśana* of Satya Sai Baba who was there for *Ugadi*. I was there with my mother and my eldest son, Rajender. After Baba's *darśana* and hearing his discourse in the evening, I went to Swami where he was then staying in Trimalgherry area, about 15 miles away. He asked me why I was there leaving my family in Vizag on *Ugadi* day. I mumbled something in concealment to the effect that I had some work in Hyderabad. Swami said that He knew I had been at Sai Baba's meeting. He said He had heard the discourse of Baba from where he was and repeated a few passages from it. The next day again we met. K.S. Dutt of Vishakhapatnam and Ramamurthy, Assistant Commissioner of Police, were also there. Swami received us with all love though we arrived much later than scheduled. He presented us with grapes and sweets, which he materialised. He said to me that I would celebrate a marriage. He presented Dutt with a raw, unhealed coconut, which he materialised and said that it was symbolic of the third eye and blessed him that his third eye might get opened. We were a little jittery because the time was up for us to catch the train which was to leave at 7:15 p.m. It was already 7:00 p.m. and we had to go some ten miles through crowded streets to the railway station, a virtually impossible feat. Sensing my anxiety Swami assured us in Biblical tone: "The train is for us. We are not for the train". After another five minutes, he said we might go. We do not know how we sped through the crowded streets at that busy hour and reached our destination. Soon as we jumped into the train with our baggage, without even locating our compartment, it whistled and started. We heaved a sign of relief. The train was for us.

After our meeting in March 1976, I could not meet Swami for a long spell of time. In the next two years, I had only one letter from Him from Puttur where, he said, he had fallen from the first floor of a house and fractured his left foot. I tried to check on his exact address several times in Hyderabad but I could not get it. Once there was a telephone call from him from Hyderabad saying that he had returned from a tour of Pondicherry and that he would shortly be going to Mysore where a tour was arranged.

A second telephone call from him was again from Hyderabad sometime in February, 1977. My wife was by then worrying herself about our daughter's marriage. I asked Swami about the marriage. He remembered Uṣā, my daughter, as the lean, tall girl who had sought his blessings two years ago and said a good alliance would be fixed and the marriage would take place after a year. As Swami said things happened.

On a few occasions, earlier, I spoke to Dora of Swami and my meetings with him and the miracles he had showed us. When I told him of Swami's arrival he readily agreed to go with me. Both of us went there. Swami materialised a *rudrākṣa* and gave it to Dora and asked him to wear it round the neck. He suddenly looked at me and asked me why I was wearing the *rudrākṣa* in the chain round my neck in a loose way allowing it to slide about the chain, without having it fixed to it immovably. I wondered how could Swami know in what way I wore the *rudrākṣa* under my shirt. Suddenly it flashed in my mind that he was always there watching me and I remembered his letter to me in 1975 that he was there to guide every one at every step spiritually.

It was late in the night when we took leave of Swami and returned home. Dora, on our way back, remarked that the trance into which Swami had slided time and again while we had been with him appeared to be as intoxicating as one or two bottles of whisky. Next day when I met Swami again he referred to this and enquired whether he appeared to be so drunk. We were stunned.

Once a local correspondent of a newspaper came to me and started asking me several questions on Swami's *līlā*s, of which he had heard. I talked to him for a long time and answered that I believed Swami was an *avatāra* and I had no hesitation to Shout it from housetops in the light of my experience. Later in the day Swami asked me what I had been doing earlier. When I told him that I had met so-and-so, he repeated to me the conversation we had had.

When I was in the United States in April-May 1978, I had several experiences of Swami's presence with me. Two such instances I wish to narrate here. Once, sitting in the lounge of Kansas City airport, I wondered how I would go about in Lawrence, my destination, where I knew no one. I heard Swami's clear voice assuring me "I am here with you, Gopala!" (*Nenunnanu Kadu Gopala*!). A little later, a stranger came to me and volunteered to take me to a hotel in Lawrence where I could stay. I had no doubt that Swamiji had come in that form and helped me.

A friend in New York told me on my way back that Swami had been embarrassed at Vishakhapatnam by some persons who had demanded to see his miracles and that he had not shown them anything. This agitated my mind a little. I had to stop in Rome *en route* for two days as the Air India flight had been cancelled. As I walked into my room, I saw a page of the *Bible* kept open. It was an Italian version with English translation side by side. It struck me strange that the book should be kept open and I presumed there was some message for me. I read it — the pages that were kept open. They narrated how Christ showed His miracles, to His disciples and to those who had faith. When Pharisees pestered Him to show the miracles, insulted Him, beat Him and spat on Him, He did not show any miracles. He said He had none. The page concluded that he who had faith could see them and experience them. Christ did not show them because they were not intended to show his power.

I did not repeat these incidents to Swami. But he asked me about them a long time later. When we were in a devotee's place in January 1979, He suddenly turned to me and said, "Gopala, why don't you tell them of your experience in America?". I was a little perplexed. I could not immediately recollect the incidents. He then continued, "Of hearing my voice in the airport and seeing the *Bible* kept open in the hotel room". I felt ashamed that I could not recollect them immediately.

Once I was to go to Hyderabad. It was a Friday. Swami was in *mauna* in a closed room in our house. Some papers which he had asked me to carry could not be collected till the last minute as I was busy with office work. Flight time was approaching and I was jittery. My young son saw my plight and said, "Daddy, why are you getting so confused, your plane will be delayed". When I asked him how he could say that, he said it was Swami who had told him so in his ear. A telephone call to airport confirmed the departure time as two hours later than the scheduled time.

I saw that Swami could become as light as a feather. In Delhi airport once he came to see me off along with a few of his other devotees. Some of the devotees started checking their weights on the weighing machine there. Swami also upon the machine and put a ten paise coin as others did. The machine's wheels did not turn. The printed card mentioning the weight did not come out. Several other persons before and after Swami were getting their cards all right. Then Swami started grumbling, "I have no weight, the machine has taken my ten paise. It should give me back my money". Saying so, he tapped on the machine and amazingly out came the ten paise coin from where the weight card was expected!

In 1976, Swami's birthday celebrations took place at Alattur in the house of Pasam Krishna Murthy. Swami cured Babu Rao of a disease pronounced incurable by leading medical practitioners. Swami assured his devotees that he would give priority to the installation of *koṭi liṅgas*. It was unanimously decided that they should all refer to Swami as 'Bhagavan Bala Siva Yogeendra Maharaj'. Swami presided over the 'Akhila Bharata Ryot Society' and the radio and press gave coverage to it. Swami went to Rangavalli to be present for the *Daśaharā* festival and then he went to Tiruttani. On Mrs. Sundaramma's invitation Swami went to Kandrika and allowed the people there to do *Abhiṣekam* to him.

At New Delhi Swami's birthday was celebrated with great devotion on 27 July 1978. Swami asked me to come there. I was planning to apply for leave and go there on my own. Then on 24 July, I received a message from Hyderabad that the state government wanted an urgent report on a particular matter to be sent in consultation with the University Grants Commission in Delhi. So I could go to Delhi on official work by 26th July, Swami's birthday celebration was at Nangia House in East Kailash. Members of the Sevā Samīti there, their families and several distinguished invitees were present on the occasion. T.A. Pai and Mrs. Pai, some judges of the Supreme Court, advocates, big businessmen and several other devotees were present. Swami materialised a big silver ring and put it on Sri Pai's finger and it was an exact fit. Swami performed *homam*. Agni (fire god) was invoked to light the *homa* without resorting to any matchstick. In the *homam* in the evening a coconut was offered in the fire. But it did not burn at all even after half an hour. Slowly the nut started breaking up when it was taken out of the fire. Swami opened it and lo! there was *pāyasam* in it. Swami distributed that small quantity of *pāyasam* to hundreds of people present there.

'*Mahimalu chupuvadu madhyamundu*', Swami always reminds us, meaning thereby that a person who shows miracles is in the middle stage of spiritual evolution. Then why does he show miracles, one wonders. We have the answer: *yogīs* who have attained *turīyāvasthā* can bring about spiritual regeneration by mere touch. But in this materialistic age, as faith in God has first to be kindled in the masses the *yogīs* make use of miracles.

Swami always warns people that miracles should not distract them from their true goal or dazzle them so much that they revere the *guru* only for his miracles. True disciples will have only *arthī* (aspiration) or *jijñasā* (thirst for knowledge) in their hearts, but never idle curiosity about the wonders the *guru* can do. Occult powers are only a very tiny superficial part of divinity and so *siddhi* has a meaning only so long as the disciple's *buddhi* (discrimination of intelligence) does not swerve from the spiritual path.

Swami's mission, as I understood it, is to dispel spiritual lethargy, awaken people into the consciousness of an all-pervasive light, the essence of godhead in every religion of the world. It is through such awakening or *tejodarśana* (Vision of Light) alone that universal peace (*viśva śānti*) is possible. *Viśva śānti teja* is another name for Swami. He is a *brahmarṣi* who has come to spread *viśva śānti* through *tejo-mārga* (the Path of Light).

Swami has not paid much attention to messages. His unique approach to the imparting of spiritual wisdom lays emphasis on the plenary experience of *tejo svarūpam* (the form of illumination) than on mere instruction. His talks and discourses are therefore simple, forthright, and precise. Swami jocularly says that he is always rough and tough hailing as he does from Cuddapah district of Andhra Pradesh. He does not mince words in revealing the truth.

The supernatural experience in which unconditioned *tejo svarūpam* is realised is *turīyāvasthā*, the fourth state of awareness beyond the three *avasthās* (states) — *jāgṛti* (wakefulness), *svapna* (dream) and *suṣupti* (deep sleep). Swami always describes this state, *turīyavasthā* as *dehattham*, *bhavattham*, *kevalātmaniranjanam* (beyond physical senses, beyond conception, as blissful existence of *ātmā* alone).

All religions refer to *jyoti* (light). *Teja*s (illumination) is a more appropriate description of that phenomenon than *jyoti*. However, the latter too is a widely accepted term. Lead us, O Lord! From darkness to light, from the unreal to the real, from death to immortality, say the Vedas. *Tejas* is the form of all. Those who realise this are worthy of their human incarnation. It is only in *tejas* that man can attain unity, and humanity enjoys everlasting happiness. This world is full of that *tejas*. All men called *avatāra*s meditate on that *tejas*. It is the form of Truth, Love and Peace.

The starting point and final destination of all religions stem from the same quest *so'ham* (that is me) of Hinduism which is echoed in Islam as, 'I am in you', and in Christianity as '*Yehova*' (It is in you). The goal of human evolution is to raise man from mundane man to divine man, who lives in *teja*s, who works in *tejas*, and who is *tejas*. *Paramātmā* is *tejosvarūpa*. Who is *paramātmā*? *Param* means the highest, the greatest, *ātmā* is that which fills all that lies between *tat* (that) and *ma* (this, the body). *Ātmā* is, therefore, that *caitanya-śakti* (conscious energy) for which there is neither a 'this' nor a 'that'.

Humanity minus Vanity is Divinity, says Swami. Total surrender is absence of vanity. *Gopīkā*s (milkmaids or shepherdesses) who surrendered their hearts to Lord Kṛṣṇa without any reserve, says Swami, are *dīpikā*s of *bhakti* (lights of devotion) and adds that all true devotees are *gopīkā*s, be they men or women. It is the presence of devotion in the heart that matters and not the sex or caste of the devotee.

Devotion is the constant remembrance of the Lord at all times and in all states. Thus, anchoring one's mind in the Lord (*paramātmā*), loving one's fellows, understanding the divinity in ourselves as the same divinity in others, and realising who one is, is *dhyāna* (meditation). Devotion has nothing to do with ritual. It is a mental state (*bhāva*). It is not mere ritual. It is constant remembrance of the idea, point or object of attention at all times and in all states. This mental attitude would some day or other culminate in devotion to the divine to God. Here too, there is no place for mere ritual. There is no restriction on one remembering God, say, that one should think of him only after bathing, and not when one is unclean in the physical sense. Purity of mind and not mere cleanliness in physical surroundings is important.

Speaking of *upavāsa* (fasting) and *jāgaraṇa* (remaining awake without sleep), Swami once wrote: "Do you know what the meaning of *upavāsa* is? *Upa* means 'nearby' and *vāsa* means, 'to live'. *Upavāsa* means to live nearby *parameśvara* not before an idol of *parameśvara*".

Swami's 108 verses in Telugu on Āñjaneya and 27 verses (*nakṣtramālā*) on *Pārvatī-patī* or Śīva are masterpieces of devotion. The ecstatic state in which they were written is apparent in the diction and thought which are their frame, and the melody and spiritual vibration with which the frame is filled. No attentive reader would miss the thrill and peace that are in them. Swami himself, singing the verses, passes into a trance, or has an incessant flow of tears down His cheeks.

'My' and 'Mine' are submerged in the greater identity of oneness with God. Swami says:

> *Vairagyam* is attachment because it is based on love and detachment, because it is not tainted by the grief caused by clinging to emotional entanglements rooted in the restrictive pattern of my family, my region or my religion. Kṛṣṇa's love has not led to the emotional bondage of the hundreds of *gopīkā*s (milkmaids or shepherdesses) who worshipped Him. It has liberated them all from the human condition of grief to the divine state of joy. It has detached them from mundane considerations and given them attachment to divinity.

Renunciation (*saṁnyāsa*) is not leaving wife, family, luxuries and comforts, and becoming an ascetic. True *saṁnyāsa* is an attitude of mind, not an external way of life. It is not a show. One should not have attachment to the things of the world but one should be in them in whatever state or position in life Lord has placed him and act his part well. *Saṁsāra* has some *sāra* (essence) of permanent happiness. That should be realised and expanded. Be in *saṁsāra* and attain happiness. Let *saṁsāra* be not in you. It is rather difficult to have happiness without being in *saṁsāra*. It is the royal path to reach the destination. The path of *saṁnyāsa* is beset with all difficulties like passing through a dense hilly forest path. He says:

> Man attached to senses is *jīva*, detached from them is *deva*.

While you meditate on the point of the meeting of the eyebrows, darkness is slowly dispelled. You begin to see one after another the colours of the rainbow: violet, indigo, blue, green yellow, orange and red. Later on, you have the vision of a *jyoti*, with the brilliance of a million suns. *Jīvanmukti* is the constant experience of this illumination. Some great souls, having attained this state, come down and spend some time for the upliftment of the world. However, their coming down to the world does not mean loss of the salvation they have attained. "Meditation", says Swami, "means passing through the middle station". What we deserve begins with our culture, moves with our effort (*sādhanā*), and results in the grace of God. *Sādhanā* is the link between what we get and God's grace. A sincere attempt at *sādhanā* without desire for results, that is, meditation attracts God's grace in the form of a *guru* or any other, and assures that the right track is followed constantly. The Swamiji says:

> *Praśānti* (peace) is God, *aśānti* (absence of peace) is man (*jīva*).

This is the dictum of Swami.

> People talk of peace of mind but it is not something that we should get from somewhere. Peace is always there in the mind. It should merely be realised. Love is foundation of peace. Peace is eternal existence. It is such love through which peace is restored and should be distributed to all. Through it, illumination should be

shown to humanity so that everlasting happiness is enjoyed.

Man has lost sight of his true nature, encompassing all energy, his Being which is of the same quality as the *paramātmā*. He puts on the body, made up of the five elements. Forgetting his own *śakti* (power), he has been labouring for thousands of years under the illusion that he is his body. In the depth of illusion, his *tamas* plays an important part. When a *sadguru* (spiritual preceptor) enlightens him, he will regain equanimity and confidence.

A real *guru*'s heart is full of motherly love. There are no barricades to that love. It is *viśva-prema* (universal love). It is with that unlimited, universal love that he always lives and he merges in it. Just as animals which live in water are born, and bred and die in water, *mahātmā*s and men of *avatāra* are born, and bred, and merge in that universal love. There are no limits to that love. Their parents and everything are the manifestation of that love. Just as a mother feels happy feeding her baby on her blood in the form of milk, *mahātmā*s enjoy using for universal well-being all their life, reputation, wealth and power, through the use of the word. A mother occasionally reprimands her children in their own interest. Likewise *mahātmā*s also reprimand people in the interest of their well-being and try to keep them on the right path. The incident of Bhagavan Ramakrishna pulling up Rani Rashmani while she was inattentive during his discourse is well known.

The world is one body. All men of all countries and of all religions are parts of that body. Whichever part is effected, the entire body has to suffer. When all the parts are healthy, the whole body appears peaceful. For example, when a tidal wave affects a part of the world, the whole world expresses its distress. Therefore, only when all men, unselfishly and in a spirit of sacrifice, discard their separate attitudes does universal peace (*viśwa-śānti*) flourish.

Bala Siva is not, as everyone thinks, in ignorance, a person with skin, flesh, blood, bones, kidneys, intestines and a physical body. He is not one with relatives like sons, friends, house, properties, and worldly things; he is not one with any illusion of birth and death and bodily emotions like anger and passion; he is not one who can be known by the *indriyas* or a desire-filled mind or *buddhi* that believes the material world to be true. He is omniscient, the Unchanging Bliss of Experience; *praśānti* and *paramānanda* unconcerned with worldly things; omnipresent in all living and non-living things in such a way that even philosophers cannot think of him as separate from themselves. Bala Siva is Brahma Siva. It is a phenomenon. Bala Siva *tattva* is *ātma tattva*. It is well illuminating. It is not dependent on anything else for its knowledge as *saccidānanda*, but is always true and existent. It is *saccidānanda*.

Every true religion broadly consists of two parts — rituals and philosophy. In the Vedas, this corresponds to *karma-kāṇḍa* and *jñāna-kāṇḍa*. It is a pity that many Hindus view rituals alone as making up the sum-total of religion. Such an attitude will result only in landing man in superstitions. On the other hand, if philosophy alone is adopted without rituals it becomes madness. So both rituals and philosophy must go hand in hand to make Hinduism a full-fledged and purposeful religion.

The Vedānta assures man that God is in man himself and that by realising one's own inner nature he recognises himself as the Eternal. Man is generally under the misapprehension that he is the body and mind and doubtful about the existence of a soul as the substratum. He does not know that he is a soul and has a body and mind. Getting over this ignorance (*ajñāna*) is possible only to man. He is born to realise this Truth. Religion is the science (subjective) of life, which enables him to achieve this. This is otherwise known as *brahma-vidyā* also. Material sciences deals with the objective world only and is empirical. Psychology deals with the mind. Spirituality or religion deals with the soul, which is the substratum of all. All religious scriptures give us a theoretical knowledge of the soul, which is the reality behind us, and also explain the various techniques through which one can have a subjective experience of the same.

The techniques through which one can gain this subjective experience have to be practised by the individual himself, after a teacher (*guru*) initiates him. For this purpose a proper teacher is to be approached, who can awake in him first his powers of creative thinking and later help him to reach the Self. To comprehend this science of life one should have faith (*śraddhā*) and devotion (*bhakti*) and do meditation (*dhyāna*). Faith is the work of the intellect and devotion is the work of the heart while meditation is the act of both.

The present-day world, which is strife-ridden, needs a universal religion that can establish common identity among mankind, conducive to universal peace. Added to this, science and technology are posing problems to public safety (skylab, etc.) Heavenly wrath (*ādidaivika*) like cyclones, tidal waves, landslides add unforeseen misery also. Protection from these is needed to save the masses from early extinction. Taking root in *sanātana dharma*, Swami Sri Bala Siva Yogendra Maharaj founded *tejo-mārga* as a counter to the above evils. This is a path which can appeal not only to the full-grown *jñānī* but to also the man who is not fully evolved. Practising on the lines advocated by him with unswerving faith one can have the vision of that conscious sea of light, thousandfold brighter than the sun, which is the same *viśvarūpadarśana* that Arjuna had through the grace of Lord Kṛṣṇa, one that settles on the individual strange calm and peace.

Immortality can be attained only by renunciation and not by work, birth or wealth. So one should adopt the above path if he is to progress spiritually. Though *jñāna* and *bhakti* are two stages in God realisation, a *jñānī* adopts the method of dispelling *māyā* to attain the Supreme while a *bhakta* adopts the method of invoking the help of *māyā* for attaining the Supreme. Of the different paths available to mankind for God realisation, *tejo-mārga* is not only the easiest but also the speediest way for the attainment of Truth. It is the jet age method for God realisation.

6

Swami Prabhupada
Interpretation of Vedānta

Monika Talapatra

Vedānta literally means the end of Vedic knowledge, and for Swami Prabhupada this knowledge is the knowledge of Kṛṣṇa. There is one Supreme Reality, One Absolute Truth, and He is to be called Kṛṣṇa. He is the root cause of everything. He is the source of each and everything. The *Vedānta sūtra, janmadyasya yataḥ,* should be explained in this light. Kṛṣṇa is the Supreme Reality from whom even the atoms have been created.

But the Absolute Truth, Kṛṣṇa is not the formless *Brahman* of the *māyāvādins*. According to the *māyāvādins*, *Brahman* is Existence, Consciousness and Bliss. *Brahman* is *nirviśeṣa*, *nirguṇa*, *nirākāra*. It has no form, no distinction in itself — it is purely impersonal. From the Advaita standpoint, *Brahman* is the sole reality. The world is an illusion, and the individual beings are nothing but *Brahman*. Swami Prabhupada vehemently opposes this *māyāvāda* ("he who follows *māyāvāda* is doomed"), and interprets Vedānta from the standpoint of Vaiṣṇava *ācāryas*, especially as advanced by Acharya Ramanuja, Acharya Madhva or Bhagavān Śrī Caitanya. Kṛṣṇa is a Person, He is the Supreme Personality; He is the Personal God. He is eternally manifested in His transcendental form — the form of *sat-cit-ānanda*. He is *saccidānanda vigraha*. Existence, Consciousness and Bliss are His qualities; He is Conscious, Existent and Blissful. He is the perfect embodiment of all divine qualities. He has the qualities of wealth, fame, strength, beauty and knowledge.

Kṛṣṇa is active; He is *sakriya*. He is the cause of the creation, maintenance and destruction of the manifested universe. He is directly and indirectly conscious of all manifestations. He is independent because there is no other cause beyond Him. He is eternally existent in His Transcendental Abode — *Goloke Brindavan*. He sits upon a golden throne and manifests His *līlā* or power with His eternal consort Radharani and is served by several milkmaids.

According to Prabhupada, Vedānta actually means knowing of Kṛṣṇa. When one understands Vedānta, he comes to know Kṛṣṇa Himself, and his own relationship with Kṛṣṇa. He who understands Kṛṣṇa, understands everything. True purpose of the *Vedānta-sūtras* is "to establish the living entity's lost relationship with Kṛṣṇa, and to execute devotional service, and ultimately achieve the highest goal of life — Love for Godhead". Everywhere in the Vedas, the term *Brahman* should be used to mean Kṛṣṇa. Acharya Prabhupada, therefore, rejects *māyāvadin*'s concept of liberation through knowledge alone. He accepts the Vaiṣṇava conception of unconditional devotion to Kṛṣṇa. Love for Kṛṣṇa or Kṛṣṇa consciousness is the one and only one way of liberation.

Prabhupada accepts Caitanya Mahāprabhu as his spiritual master. According to him, Śrī Caitanya Mahāprabhu is an incarnation of Kṛṣṇa. He sincerely believes and advocates that Mahāprabhu is the real embodiment of Lord Kṛṣṇa. Kṛṣṇa really took form in Śrī Caitanya. Swami Prabhupada quotes from the *Bhagavad Gītā* to prove that Caitanya Mahāprabhu is really Kṛṣṇa Caitanya, Kṛṣṇa personified in Mahāprabhu. In the effulgence lies the real Being — The Personal Kṛṣṇa. The sun is known when we cross beyond its rays, sunshine. Rays are formless but the sun is not. The *māyāvādins* are awed by the formless effulgence, glaring halo, and think the Supreme Reality to be impersonal; the personal nature of Absolute Truth remains ever unknown to them. A hymn in the *Īśopaniṣad*, as Prabhupada says, is a clear proof of this Personal nature of *Brahman*.

O my Lord, Sustainer of all that lives, your face is covered by your dazzling Light, glaring halo. Kindly remove the covering and show yourself to your pure devotee.

Swami Prabhupada advances further. Supreme Reality is Personal, *Brahman* is Kṛṣṇa, but what is the metaphysical status of the world and *jīva*? Is the world an illusion? Are *jīva*s nothing but *Brahman* Himself?

The answer to both is an empathic 'No'.

Kṛṣṇa creates the universe. Each and everything of the world has its root cause in God. All spiritual and material world emanates from Him. He is manifested in everything. But we must remember that it is only a partial manifestation. We are created by Him no doubt, but are never equal to Him. World, no doubt, has its source in *Brahman*. It is never an illusion, but it is not a permanent one. World is *anitya* but not *māyā*. The *jīva*s are sons of Kṛṣṇa, He is our Father; the living entity is eternally related with Kṛṣṇa in the relationship of Son and Father, Servant and Master. He is the soul of all individual Souls — but still, He is transcendent to us all. This is, in short, as Prabhupada says, the teaching of Vedānta. Study of Vedānta gives us knowledge of Kṛṣṇa. It arouses in us Kṛṣṇa consciousness.

Hence, according to Prabhupada, we should accept Caitanya as God; Lord Caitanya is Kṛṣṇa with the external features of Rādhārānī. Śrī Caitanya is God. Therefore worshipping him will lead us to God-realisation. Mahāprabhu, as Prabhupada says, shows the path to God. It is not the path of *jñāna-yoga*, *karma-yoga* or *haṭha-yoga* but it is the path of *bhakti-yoga*, the uncompromised devotion to Kṛṣṇa. It is the pure love for God. Here we surrender everything to God. When we have in our lives nothing but Kṛṣṇa, when He becomes the sole supreme object of Love, we feel the transcendental love. At this moment only, we realise Kṛṣṇa, the Supreme Personality of Godhead. This is Kṛṣṇa consciousness. This is our highest goal. To achieve this, we have to chant Kṛṣṇa *mantra* with our whole heart. Non-stop chanting of the *mantra* and dancing with it is the only way to be merged in the vast ocean of Kṛṣṇa consciousness.

hare kṛṣṇa hare kṛṣṇā, kṛṣṇā kṛṣṇā hare hare.
hare rāma hare rāmā, rāmā rāmā hare hare.

This teaching, as Prabhupada says, has come by discipline — succession or *paramparā*. In the *Śrīmad Bhāgavatam*, Kṛṣṇa imparted this knowledge into the heart of Brahmā, the first created being in the universe. Brahmā imparted it to Nārada and Nārada passed it to Vyāsadeva. From Vyāsadeva, Madhvācārya got the message and from Madhvācārya, the knowledge came down to Mādhavānanda Purī, then to Īśvara Purī and from him to Caitanya Mahāprabhu.

Swami Prabhupada, therefore, accepts the *Śrīmad Bhāgavatam* to be the authoritative scripture of his philosophy. His philosophy is based on the conception of a Personal God, the Kṛṣṇa — the One Absolute Truth. According to him, the *māyāvadins* cannot grasp the full essence of Vedānta. Supreme Reality is both impersonal and personal. The impersonality is the glow, the radiance and the effulgence of the Personal Being. Beyond loving service, it is to be understood that he is adverse to the study of Vedānta, and to the understanding of the Supreme Personality of Godhead.

Hence to Prabhupada, there should be no distinction of caste and creed where Kṛṣṇa devotion is concerned. Pure devotion is the only criteria. That which matters is only love for God. Only a pure devotee can be the spiritual master, whether he is born in a brāhmaṇa family or not. Lord Caitanya made no distinction between a brāhmaṇa and a śūdra. He took food in Vaidya's house. This concept, as Prabhupada, says, will stop all bickering and unnecessary hatred among different castes. Human society will undergo a qualitative change. We will have the social bond of spiritual love.

Sri Prabhupada wanted to spread the teaching of Mahāprabhu throughout the world. He established several centres for Kṛṣṇa consciousness, the ISKCON (International Society for Krishna Consciousness) in different countries. Within a short span of time, this new interpretation of Vedānta and this message of

Kṛṣṇa *mantra* was imparted to millions of people all over the world. The message is really a universal science of God Realisation. There are different religions; God's holy name may differ from religion to religion and rituals, doctrines and customs may differ from one religion to another. But the point is, how much do we love God. Real religion means to learn to love God. And how to love God is the sum and substance of Prabhupada's teaching.

In Calcutta, Swami Prabhupada established the ISKCON centre in Albert Road. Here devotees, followers, common people — all flock together to get some peace of mind, to chant the *hare kṛṣṇa mantra*, and to be merged in the sea of Kṛṣṇa devotion. ISKCON's teaching of unconditional devotion to Kṛṣṇa will make human society experience a new Light of spiritual life — which will open the field of activities for a pure soul.

7

Swamī Bhuteshananda: Vedānta

Monika Talapatra

SWAMI Bhuteshananda, the President of Belur Ramakrishna Math and Mission, Belur, West Bengal is the guiding force for millions of people in India and abroad. The main centre of Ramakrishna order is located in Belur, but its branches are scattered all over the world. Bhuteshanandaji is the chief personality, the guiding force of the whole Ramakrishna *saṁgha* or order.

Much of his earlier life is unknown. He was born in 1901 in the village of Somsara in Bankura district of West Bengal. After graduating in Philosophy from Government. Sanskrit College of Calcutta, he joined Ramakrishna Math. His *guru* was Swami Saradanand, a direct disciple of Ramakrishna Paramahamsa. Here his name was Priya Caitanya. In 1928 he became a monk. As a monk, his activities were vast and varied. He was the chief of the Dhaka centre from 1930-32. After that, he became a teacher of world religious studies in Chennai and Mysore. In 1936, he went to Shillong and served among the poor, the scheduled castes and tribes of the whole eastern zone of India. From 1945 to 1966, he was the chief of Rajkot centre. As a vice-president of the Ramakrishna *saṁgha*, he stayed for a long time in Jogodyan, one of the main centres of the Mission in Kolkata.

In January 1989, after the expiry of Swami Gambhirananda, he took the charge of Ramakrishna Math and Mission as its twelfth President. Swami Bhuteshananda is a vastly learned man and he has to his credit lots of books written either in Bengali or in English. Among his works, there are *Śrī Rāmākr̥ṣṇa and*

Kathāmṛta Prasango (five volumes), *Muṇḍakopaniṣad*, *Saraṇāgati*, *Upaniṣad and Today*'s *Human Beings*, *Śrī Rāmākṛṣṇa O Yuga Dharmā*, *Thoughts on Spiritual Life* and others.

As a *guru*, he neither preaches mysticism nor demonstrates any miracle. His mysticism lies in the fact that he rises high above the worldly limitations, becomes one with the Absolute, but still feels for the layman and tries his best to show him the path to salvation. His actions of miracle, if we can really call it miracle in the literal sense of the term, are actions of service and help to the people in distress. Be there a flood, an epidemic, or a draught, the Ramakrishna Mission people arrive there at once with all aids and helps. No time is lost, no question of caste and creed is asked, no problem of money or manpower — the Ramakrishna Mission people, under the guidance of Bhuteshanandaji, are present there immediately. If this is not a miracle what else can be called a miraculous act? His speech bestows bliss, his touch brings peace, his mere presence fills the atmosphere with joy and happiness. If this is not a miracle, what else can it be? He is the lighted soul to enlighten another soul; He is the lamp from which other lamps are lighted.

At this age of 95, Swamiji has innumerable disciples both in India and abroad. According to him, spiritual knowledge is a gift from the *guru* to the disciple — and it has to be earned through humility and spirit of service. *Guru* shows the disciple the path of religion. It is necessary that the disciple must have full faith in his *guru*, but nevertheless, says Bhuteshananda, we should not take *guru*s for granted and should not follow them blindly. The followers must test, they must critically analyse what the *guru* has to preach. But this rational approach is not scepticism; it is not suspicion. It is the intellectual love of God that arises when the mind becomes free from all doubts and dogmas, and awakens to the true light of knowledge, imparted by the *guru* to his disciple. Swamiji never advises mere blind faith on *guru*s but the *guru* is to be "understood as a guide who helps us gradually to proceed along the spiritual path and who in case of confusion arouses higher knowledge in mind". But again, Swamiji warns us, once the *guru* is selected, he must be taken as next to God, as the living link between God and man.

But exactly what is his views on philosophy, religion and morality? On philosophy his view is not different from that of Ramakrishna and Vivekananda. It is the philosophy of Vedānta, but not in its traditional interpretations. Ramakrishna Paramahamsa advocated a single religion, true for all mankind. Its prerequisites were taken from Vedānta. The Absolute is the Supreme truth, it is the principle of existence, consciousness, and bliss; it is free from all internal distinctions at the same time. Ramakrishna rejected the concept that the world was illusory. He defended the importance of public activities.

According to Vivekananda, perfection is inherent in man. Every man is potentially perfect. Every man has divinity in him. It is the *ātman*, the Self, which is permanent and ever free. This Divinity is one and only one, the *ātman*, the consciousness and the sole existence. Every human being, rather, each and every being of this universe, is a manifestation of this all-pervading divinity. The same *ātman*, the same consciousness is inherent in everybody; hence there is no distinction and difference among us. We are all the same, we are all one, the one omnipresent Supreme Soul which is inherent in everybody. According to Vivekananda, this wonderful idea of oneness, this realisation of sameness should be preached for the elevation of human race. We should always remember 'I am God myself' and each and everybody is 'God himself'. Hence he said his goal would be not the intellectual discussion of theories but practical service to mankind. By serving mankind, we serve God. Vivekananda taught the fundamental unity of mankind that is preached by Vedānta philosophy. But it is not the intellectual Vedānta, but practical Vedānta, as he himself called it. He translated the message into practice all through his life and actions.

Swami Bhuteshananda advances further. He calls the Divine power God and paves the way for God realisation. The more the divine qualities are manifested, the more God will be real to us. As we realise God, we become God-like. According to him, complete realisation means complete identification with God, or elimination of separateness from God. It means an intuitive experience of the ultimate ground of all existence. Here, the seer and the seen, the subject and the object become one; the individual Self merges completely in the Absolute Self. Swamiji quotes from Upaniṣads:

> Just as water falling into a vast sheet of water becomes one with it, so also becomes the Self of a contemplative man who has realised God.

We are finite, limited and imperfect beings. It arouses in us the idea of an Infinite, Unlimited and Perfect Being. This perfect infinite being is our goal. We may call this perfect being God, or may not call it thus, but one thing is certain. The urge to transcend the limitation is common to everybody. Even the atheist has this urge. When we make the attainment of Divinity our goal, we become religious. Our spiritual progress corresponds with this attainment of Divinity. The moment we reach the goal, the moment we realise God, we lose our individuality, cross our limitations, and get rid of our imperfections. We realise, there is one and only one Universal Self, the *ātman* — the Existence, Consciousness and Bliss. There is no duality; my individuality, my ego is a creation of my own ignorance. The moment we dispel with our ignorance, the truth shines by itself. I am nothing but He (*aham brahmāsmi*), only He (*Brahman*) is there (*brahmaiva kevalam*). Bhuteshananda has favoured this Advaitic standpoint as God-realisation.

But the question is how to achieve the goal in life? What is the path to realise God? Swami Bhuteshananda emphasises the need for practical training. Theoretical discussions are endless and they lead us nowhere. They become fruitful only when they are based on moral and spiritual training. Swamiji admits that each of the threefold paths of *jñāna*, *karma* and *bhakti* can lead us to the ultimate goal.

Herein lies the distinction between Śaṅkara's philosophy and Bhuteshananda's theory. According to Śaṅkara, *mokṣa* (salvation) comes through knowledge and knowledge alone.

There is no need of *karma* or *bhakti*. But the monks of Ramakrishna Mission realised that too much of this idea will make people aloof from the world. Hence they put stress on *karma* or actions but it should be *niṣkāma karma*, actions without the hope of any consequences. *Bhakti* also should have a place; we should have prayers and rituals, but the prayer should be a direct communication with God. Swami agrees with his *guru* Sri Ramakrishna; he says,

> Whatever be the concept of God, if you pray with all earnestness, He will reveal himself to you.

This is a very practical way of telling that we need not bother about different paths to realise God. Each and every path arrives at the same Truth; any person can follow any of these paths and realise God. If this is the philosophy of life, if each and every being is the manifestation of One Ultimate Reality, then surely in human beings, the manifestation would be at its best. Therefore, according to Bhuteshananda, service to God is service to mankind. If each and every human being is a manifestation of God, then instead of worshipping images of stone or clay, why are we not worshipping human beings? 'I am He', 'You are That' — if all these Upaniṣadic dictums are true, let us serve human beings as our God. He says, religion is nothing but service to mankind. This is the essence of religion in Bhuteshananda's theory.

In spite of all services to mankind, Swami Bhuteshananda reminds as:

> One should remember that it is not a merely social service movement. A social service organisation has got the idea of improving the lot of the people only economically or materially or at best by improving their intellect. Ours is a service to help a man manifest his inner divinity. We serve Śiva (God) in *jīva*. Unless a man is established in the infinite spiritual strength within him, his problems will not be fully solved.
>
> — *Thoughts on Spiritual Life*

Let us repeat once again Vivekananda's preaching. First let us be God and then help others to be gods. Works, worship, psychic control or philosophy — any or all combined together may lead us to the goal and this is the whole of religion. Doctrines or dogmas, rituals or books, temples or forms are but secondary details; the motto will be salvation of self and the good of the world.

According to Bhuteshananda, this motto is a perfect combination of philosophy and religion. Two half-truths combined together give the full truth. Theory and practice, spiritual striving and practical training, religion and morality should be blended together to get the goal. The Ramakrishna Math and the Ramakrishna Mission blend the twin ideals together. (The Ramakrishna Maṭh and The Ramakrishna Mission combined together form the Ramakrishna Sangha or Order). The Ramakrishna Math emphasises the spiritual side while the Mission emphasises the practical side. Keeping in mind the goal of attaining perfection in life, monks as well as common people from all walks of life co-operate together to spread the idea of service to the whole mankind. Throughout the world, Ramakrishna Mission has got about 130 centres, but still, feels Swamiji, we cannot work as effectively and as extensively as we would like to do.

> Ideas are there, only they have to be made effective in life. And that can be done only by people who take to them not merely as a sort of speculation but as a way of life. People are seeking these ideas not merely for the betterment of their material life but also for enriching their whole existence.

The mission of Bhuteshananda is to reach and preach everywhere so that he and his disciples are not only doing service to themselves, but through their spiritual striving and dedication are helpful to others also.

Swami Bhuteshananda's teaching is relevant and most appropriate in today's society. Vedānta philosophy does not mean aloofness from the material world; neither does it mean an ascetic life of the monks. Rather, the world and God all are blended together to make an integrated whole. One and only one Reality is there: the Absolute God and everything in the universe is a manifestation of this Ultimate Reality. To make people realise this truth is the task of religion. And all religions are true: "The Lord of one religion is the Lord of all religions". True religion is to serve mankind. Service to mankind makes us religious and elevates us above the narrow limitations to the true realisation of God. It may come from any religion. All religions lead to the same goal as different rivers merge in the same ocean from different directions. It may be Hinduism, Christianity, or Islam but the ideal is the same. This tolerance to all religions is what we earnestly need today. Our norm in morality should be not 'my egoistic good' but the 'altruistic good' because we are all the same. There is no distinction of caste, creed or sex and no distinctions of countries or nations; we are all human beings — all the manifestations of one universal Self. But underlying all this religion and morality, there is the flame of philosophical aspiration — we must transcend our limitations and be one with the absolute whole.

8

Biswanatha Baba

Viśuddhādvaitavāda

Nimita Kar & Bijayananda Kar

LATE Biswanatha Baba is regarded as the recent exponent of Mahimā *dharmā* and *darśana*. As a matter of fact it is he who has for the first time tried to discuss the philosophical background of the Mahimā *dharma*. Though Mahimā Swami is said to be the original founder of this dhārmic cult and his viewpoint is supposed to have been conveyed through his disciples and supporters in different times, the devotional prayer-verses composed by Bhīma Bhoi, which are otherwise most attractive and popular among the masses, are greatly responsible for the spread and development of Mahimā cult both in and outside Orissa. This dhārmic cult has been quite popular among the innocent, non-sophisticated tribal and other downtrodden masses and has not acquired considerable support among the intellectuals and somewhat alerted members of the society.

Attempts have been made by some modern writers to view Mahimā *dharma* in terms of certain framework based on classical *darśana*. Scholars like N.N. Vasu have viewed Mahimā as a minor form of movement in the background of *bauddha-darśana*.[1] The researcher, Arto Ballav Mohanty, while editing the *Madhucakra* of Bhīma Bhoi, has commented on Mahimā *dharma* as having the foothold of Advaita *darśana*.[2] Both these writers are obviously neither recognised experts in classical *darśana* nor exponents of Mahimā *darśana*, as approved and recognised by the Mahimā cult. They seem to have arrived at their respective remarks observing certain similar terms and expressions used in the literature covering Mahimā as well as Buddhism and Advaita.

It is Brahma Avadhut Biswanatha Baba who being the head, *adhyakṣa* of the Mahimā *gaddī* of Joranda (the main centre of Mahimā *dharma*) has been endowed with authority to bring out the rationale of this cult. Having travelled widely in order to spread and propagate the message of Mahimā and being a scholar in Sanskrit as well as classical Indian culture, he has fully utilised his research in explaining the philosophical background of Mahimā *dharma*, an important accomplishment which has not been worked out before. This indeed is a great contribution and it is more or less accepted and unopposed by the adherents of Mahimā dhārmic order.

Though Biswanatha Baba has written profusely on Mahimā cult, his major contribution is the *Sarva-Veda-Vedānta-Sār-Tattva Śiromaṇi — Āloka Param Brahma Darśana*, which elaborately narrates the Mahimā *dharma darśana*. This treatise is published in two big volumes, each containing more than 600 pages.[3] Besides elucidating the salient features of Āloka Mahimā *dharma*, Biswanatha Baba has tried to locate its distinctive honorific place in the pedestal of Vedānta *darśana*. That Āloka or Mahimā point of view is substantially rooted in Vedānta *darśana* is clear from his characterisation of Āloka *darśana* as *Veda-Vedānta-Sāra Tattva Śiromaṇi*. It is this very significant point that facilitates the reader to locate the Mahimā *dharma-darśana* in the classical Indian philosophic tradition.[4] The Mahimā *dharma* rests upon the admittance of *ātman/Brahman* as the only foundational principle. The aim of this *dharma* is for the realisation of this *tattva* alone (*ātmabodha/jñāna*).

The Vedāntic concept of *ātman* has been interpreted variously by later scholars of eminence (*ācāryas*). Apart from the well-known commentary on Vedānta by Śaṅkara, i.e., Advaita Veda, the philosophical tradition in India is quite rich in having Viśiṣṭā-dvaitavāda (Rāmānuja), Dvaitavāda (Madhva), Dvaitādvaitavāda (Nimbārka), Śuddhādvaitavāda (Vallabha) and Acintyabhedābhedavāda (Baladeva Vidyābhuṣaṇa). All these six *ācāryas* including Śaṅkara have tried to vindicate their respective *darśanas* by way of commenting upon the well-known *prasthānatrayī* in the Vedāntic tradition, namely, the Upaniṣads, the *Brahma-sūtra* and the *Bhagavad Gītā*. Even if Śrī Caitanya is well acknowledged as the advocate of the doctrine of Acintyabhedābheda, he in his lifetime was not recognised in the *Dharma-darśana* tradition as the representative-*ācārya* for not presenting a commentary on the *prasthānatrayī*. That lacuna was fulfilled by his great follower, Baladeva who composed the famous *Govinda Bhāṣya* and was able to place Acintyabhedābheda on a dignified footing.

After Śrī Caitanya's devotional (*bhaktika*) rendering of Vedānta in the sixteenth century, one does not notice such *ācārya*-tradition in the field of *darśana*. However, in the modern period, one finds in Sri Aurobindo an original interpretation of Vedānta (though primarily rooted on Advaitic vision) which is termed as *Purṇādvaita* (Integral non-dualism). This is well exhibited in his famous work, *The Life Divine*, an independent work though not a commentary on *prasthānatrayī*. Swami Vivekananda also, in his works, has tried to present a new outlook on classical Advaita Vedānta by emphasising the practical implication of that *darśana* which is acknowledged usually as a Neo-Vedānta.

In a similar manner, Biswanatha Baba's *Ālekha Param Brahma Darśanam* is an independent work and is claimed to be the exposition of a distinct type of Advaitism. This treatise, even though not a commentary on *prasthānatrayī*, is a detailed presentation of Viśuddhādvaitavāda. Biswanatha Baba, while presenting this distinct form of Advaitism, has tried carefully to emphasise its distinction from the Advaitavāda of Śaṅkara.[5]

According to him, Śaṅkara has not given any emphasis on what he calls as *śaraṇa darśana* while advocating *ātma-jñāna*. On the contrary, Mahimā Swami has duly emphasised the role of *śaraṇa* in *satya*-Mahimā based on *viśuddhātma-jñāna-bhakti yoga*. Besides this, Śaṅkara, despite his clear emphasis on *nirguṇa* and *nirākāra* Advaitavāda, has not been able to keep himself away from the inconsistent practices of worshipping a number of *deva*s and *devī*s. The defence of this procedure by means of taking recourse to what is usually called as *vyāvahārika*, as distinct from *pāramārthika*, is not viewed as convincing. It is the sanction of worship of different deities that, Biswanatha Baba thinks, keeps the Advaita *darśana* of Śaṅkara much away from Advaitism that is only centred around the *niṣprapañca*, *nirviśeṣa*, *nirañjana Brahman*. On the contrary, it gave an indirect boost at least to the different *dvaitādvaitin*s in later times who some way or the other remained confined to what Biswanath Baba terms as *saguṇa deva devī upāsanā*, i.e., *mūrtipūjā*. In that way, the real original Advaita point of view goes to oblivion. Biswanatha Baba thinks that it is Mahimā Swami who has therefore rightly drawn our attention to only *Ālekha Brahma Śaraṇāgati* and thus is the advocate of Viśuddhādvaitavāda. In this connection he tries to give his interpretation a traditional footing and quotes an Upaniṣadic line from *Nirālamba Mahāvākya Ratnāvalī* which reads as *deva manuṣya-dyupāsanākama samkapobandaḥ*. He even goes further to cite certain passages from *Bhagavad Gītā*, *Pañca-daśī* and Śaṅkara's *Nirañjanāṣṭakam* to justify his own point of view that sets aside idol-worship from Advaita *darśana*.[6]

Another important point of departure of Biswanatha Baba from Śaṅkara's Advaita is his exclusion of the concept of *māyā* and inclusion of the concept of Mahimā. Śaṅkara, according to him, has misrepresented Advaitavāda by introducing *māyāvāda*. By accepting *māyā* or *avidyā* as the cause of world-creation, Śaṅkara is forced to admit two principles, *Brahman* and *avidyā*, which Biswanatha Baba thinks as quite inconsistent to the prior acceptance of Advaita or non-dualism. The fundamental tenet of Advaitavāda is said to be misconceived by declaring both *ātman* as *nirguṇa* and *jagat* or world as existing due to *avidyā*.

It may be pointed out, in this connection, that Vallabhācārya had advanced Śuddhādvaitavāda or pure Non-dualism in the fifteenth century.[7] He also had regarded pure Advaita as undefiled by *māyā*. His follower, Giridhara's words in this context are worth noting:

> *māyā sambandaha rahitam śuddham ityucyate budhaiah*
>
> — *Śuddhādvaita Mārttaṇḍa*

This clearly suggests that according to this school of thought, pure Advaitism excludes *māyā*. The *jagat* is not unreal but is declared to be the real manifestation of Īśvara who is identified with Śrī Kṛṣṇa. Here there is no difference maintained between *Brahman* and Lord Kṛṣṇa. By way of making a subtle distinction between the concepts of *jagat* and *saṁsāra* the *śuddhādvaitins* maintain that while *jagat* is real and not illusory, the *saṁsāra*, i.e., the cycle of birth and death ceases to exist after the sensation of ignorance and the attainment of *śuddha-jñāna*. As regards creation, the Vallabhaites maintain that it is possible out of the grace of the Lord (*pūṣaṇam tadanugrahaḥ*) and that is why this Śuddhādvaita school is named as *puṣṭi-mārga*.

It may be remarked that Biswanath Baba, in his Viśuddhādvaitavāda, accepts Advaita *Brahman* as devoid of all characterisations. In this sense *māyā* as *śakti* of *Brahman* and the cause of creation, is inadmissible. Instead of *māyā*, he emphasises on Mahimā in the Advaitic framework. *Mahimā* does not mean another independent *tattva*. It also does not stand for unreality or falsity like that of *māyā*. It is the *Brahman* which is regarded as *mahima* (wonderful greatness) as such; creation is not due to *māyā* but is due to *mahimā* of *Brahman*. *Mahimā* is not an attribute but constitutes the very being of *Brahman*. As *Brahman* is regarded as *sat-cit-ānanda svarūpa* so also it is taken as *satya mahimā Svarupa*. Biswanath Baba, in this regard, has quoted passages from various *Upaniṣads* like *Śvetāśvatara*, *Kaṭha* and *Chāndogya* to justify the emphasis of *mahimā* so far as the Vedāntic *ātma-tattva* is concerned.[8] Advaitism that excludes *māyā-vāda* and includes *mahimā-vāda* is viewed to be pure (*viśuddha*) according to him. Even if Advaita means the admittance of one non-dual principle, i.e., *Brahman* alone and diversity (*nānātva*) in any form is inadmissible in this regard, the Viśuddhādvaitavāda accommodates the creation of the world consisting of multiplicity. It is said that the world creation — is possible out of *Brahman* (the highest Lord) because of his wonderful greatness (*mahimā*). And, as such, there is no deviation from the track of pure non-dualism. Even if there are diversities in creation, these do not have any separate independent being or status apart from *Brahman* and, therefore, the non-duality of *Brahman* is least affected by the admittance of such theory of creation. In this connection, Biswanatha Baba quotes passages from some Upaniṣads for the purpose of corroboration.[9]

From the aforesaid discussion, it seems fairly clear that Viśuddhādvaitavāda has the following distinctive features. Advaita *Brahman*, though *nirguṇa* and *nirākāra*, can be the object of meditation or *upāsanā*. For the attainment of *mokṣa*, one has to surrender to Ālekha *Brahman*, the *mahimā svarūpa prabhu*. The world-creation is viewed as not illusory (*māyika*) but is real being directly possible due to *Brahman*. It is *Brahman* alone, which is the cause of creation and creation is not different but His own manifestation in another setting. The worship of different *deva*s and *devī*s is not warranted because, in Advaita, there cannot be any scope for duality or plurality. *Brahman*, as the highest Lord without any form, size or shape, is alone real. So the worship of plural deities is discouraged. However, instead of *pūjā*, the devotional meditations and prayers to Mahimā *Brahman* are very much acceptable in order to sustain the *bhakti* element within the Advaita fold. This type of doctrine of Advaita is pure and unalloyed as it is not mixed up with the element of *māyā* and also is not accommodative of worship of a number of *deva*s and *devī*s (i.e., idol-worship). So far as the inclusion of *bhakti* and *upāsanā* of *Brahman* is concerned, the Mahimā point of view seems to have inspiration from *bhakti-miśra-advaita-jñāna yoga* as introduced by Sridhar Swami who belongs to this part of the country (being the 10th Śaṅkarācārya of Govardhan Maṭh at Purī) and who, most possibly, inspired the Orissan Vaiṣṇavite thinkers to propagate *jñāna-miśra-bhakti-yoga* with which the Mahimaites seem to have close affinity. Of course, in Mahimā, it is encouraged in the background of the Advaitic framework, while in Orissan Vaiṣṇavism (*pañca-śākhā*) it is at the background of Vaiṣṇava form of Vedānta.[10]

Such an attempt to pinpoint the distinctive position of the doctrine of Viśuddhādvaitavāda is no doubt a commendable task performed by Biswanatha Baba. He has been able to place this dhārmic cult on an independent dārśanic footing. In his writings, he has carefully shown its distinction by way of comparing as well as contrasting it from other classical Vedānta *darśanas*. He even, as indicated before, cites number of Śruti and Smṛti passages to corroborate his stand. That Advaita *Brahman* is also Mahimā *svarūpa* is well traceable in some Vedic and Upaniṣadic sources.[11]

Reference

1. Vasu, N.N., *The Modern Buddhism and its Followers in Orissa*, pp. 150-72.
2. Mohanty, A.B. (ed.), Preface to Bhīma Bhoi's *Cautisa Madhucakra*, 1962.
3. Baba, Biswanatha, *Sarva Veda-Vedānta Sāratattva-Śiromoṇi Ālekha Parambrahma Darśanam* (in two vols. *Pūrvārdha* and *Uttarārdha*), 1968.
4. In this manner, Biswanatha Baba seems to have cleared the passage for the later scholars to come to the valid conclusion that the Mahimā dhārmic-cum-dārśanic movement is based on the classical Indian religio-philosophical tradition. Here the views of scholars like Late Prof. P. Mukherjee, *History of Medieval Vaiṣṇavism in Orissa*, Calcutta, 1941; Late Dr. (Miss.) A. Eschmann, 'Spread, Organisation and Cult of Mahimā Dharma' in *Mahimā Dharma and Darśana*, pp.7-11, Panda, D. (ed.), 1972; C.R. Das, *Studies in Medieval Religion and Literature in Orissa* in *Visva-Bharati Annals*, vol.III, 1950; B. Kar (the present author), '*Biswanatha Baba on Mahimā and Advaita*' in *Mahimā Dharma and Darśana*, *op.cit.*, pp.38-9; and Ishita Bandopadhyaya, *Religion and Society in Orissa: Mahimā Dharma in the Nineteenth and Twentieth centuries*, an unpublished

Ph.D. thesis in History at the Calcutta University, 1994 may be referred to.

5. Baba, Biswanatha, 'Satya-Mahimā Dharma-Darśana Tattva' in *Mahimā Dharma and Darśana, op. cit.*, pp. i-xiii.
6. *Mahimā Dharma and Darśana*, pp. xi-xii.
7. Vide, *Anu-Bhāṣya*, Vallabha's commentary on *Brahma-Sūtra*.
8. Vide, '*Satya-Mahimā Dharma-Darsana Tattva*'.
9. *Satya-Mahimā Dharma-Darśana Tattva*, pp. iii-iv.
10. Vide Mukherjee, P., *History of Medieval Vaisnavism in Orissa, op.cit.*, and Kar, B., 'The Religious Philosophy of Mahimā Goswami and his School' in *Bharati*, July, 1969. The latter is reprinted in a modified form with a new title 'The Philosophy of Mahimā Dharma' in *Major Trends in Orissan Philosophy*, 1989.
11. Vide '*Satya-Mahimā Dharma-Darsana Tattva*', *op. cit.*, pp. iv-v.

9

Gandhiji: Ideal of Non-violence

T. Padma

THE enigma of modern life is that unprecedented scientific and technological progress is juxtaposed with unheard of civilisational sepsis. Owing to the growth of violence in every walk of life, man, while enjoying undreamt-of comforts, is denied even a modicum of peace and security. Whatever may be the couse of origin of this ubiquitous violence — poverty, privation, political instability or psychological perversion — it invariably leaves in its wake broken homes and bruised psyches. These, in turn, serve as breeding grounds for all sorts of anti-social activities. The only way out of this vicious circle seems to be a return to the Gandhian ideal of non-violence. The anomaly of the demolition of the Berlin Wall and of the Iron Curtain seeming to unleash more violence instead of promoting peace has an answer only in the Gandhian Ethic of Means and Goals; stable peace can never be achieved by recourse to violence. Non-violence is no longer an option. It is an imperative.

Non-violence can be cited as the quintessential teaching of scriptures the worldover. Philosophers like Lao-Tsu of China and Socrates of Greece, not to mention the Pacific Quakers among others, have all extolled the inner equipoise promoted by the practice of non-violence. However, the first person to use it as a strategy of resistance was the American writer, Thoreau. Inspired by his chance reading of an English rendering of the *Gītā*, he single handedly launched a peaceful non-co-operation campaign against America's war with Mexico. This had a profound impact on Tolstoy's credo of non-resistance to evil. Interestingly, it is Tolstoy's gifting of a copy of Thoreau's Civil Disobedience that enthused Gandhi to launch his First Civil Disobedience Movement in South Africa. Gandhi's effective implementation of the tactic of non-violence has gained for him the reverential title *mahātma*, while his simple attire, abstemious ways, unassuming air and easy accessibility to, and caring concern for, the rich and the poor alike have earned for him the loving appellation *bāpūjī*. Mahatma Gandhi has, by virtue of his charismatic personality, saintly bearing and political astuteness, rightly become a trail-blazer for illustrious leaders — like Martin Luther King in the past and Nelson Mandela now.

A discussion of Gandhian non-violence invariably involves a consideration of its connection with his concept of Truth. In Indian thought, *satya* and *ahiṁsā* are alike rated high and in almost identical terms: *Satyānnāsti paro dharmaḥ* (there is no law higher than truth) and *ahiṁsā paramo dharmāḥ* (non-jury is the supreme law). The working Document prepared by the UNESCO's Division of Philosophy for the 1969 Symposium on Gandhi clarifies the nature of the interlinkage of *satya* and *ahiṁsā*:

> The mere fact of their being linked would seem to suggest that truth and non-violence are not to be thought of as general concepts but that truth is what expresses itself in non-violent action and non-violence is what advances the cause of truth. (351-52)

For quite some time Gandhi's non-violent demonstrations went by the name of passive resistance. To counter the possibility of non-violence being misunderstood as a philosophy of the weak, Gandhi invited an adequate synonym from readers of *Indian Opinion* and even announced a prize for the best suggestion. Maganlal was awarded the prize for his suggesting the name *sadāgraha* (*sat* = truth, *āgraha* = firmness). Gandhi changed it to *satyāgraha*.

Another way of emphasising the roots of the Gandhian ideal of non-violence in the Hindu tradition is to view this ideal as an integral part of his self-imposed agenda of discipline comprising vows known as *vratas*. *Vrata*, as pointed out by V. Raghavan, is an ancient basic word in the Vedas that signified

> the practical aspect of the perception of *Rta*, the divine or cosmic order or law; *Vrata* is acting in conformity to it. (115)

The vows Gandhi enjoined on the inmates of the Sabarmati Ashram are vows mentioned in Patañjali's *Yogasūtras*: *ahiṁsā*, *satya*, *āsteya*, *brahmacarya* and *aparigraha*. Gandhi was fond of remarking that the precepts of the *Yogasūtras* were endorsed by all the Upaniṣads. *Īśopaniṣad* was his favourite and he often quoted its opening verse, which in Radhakrishnan's rendering runs as:

> (Know that) all this, whatever moves in this moving world, is enveloped by God. Therefore, find your enjoyment in renunciation; do not covet what belongs to others. (567)

Like other national leaders of the time, like Tilak and Sri Aurobindo, Gandhi also relied on the *Gītā* for guidance and spiritual solace. Tilak found in the *Gītā* a clarion call for duty while Sri Aurobindo saw in it the triumph of good over evil. What appealed most to Gandhi in the *Gītā* was the ideal of commitment to action with *sthita-prajña* or unwavering mental equipoise. Gandhi sincerely followed the *Gītā*'s gospel of disinterested action or *anāsakti-yoga*. In his *Autobiography*, Gandhi reverentially refers to the *Gītā* as his dictionary of daily reference (195).

Gandhian non-violence is more than a principle. It is a monitor of action. He was primarily a *karma-yogī* and the spirit behind the principle of non-violence lent his actions a peculiar piquancy. The practice of non-violence was for Gandhi a life-long pursuit, demanding persistent inquiry, instructive even through apparent failures and enlightening through the dictates of the inner voice, *antaḥkaraṇa*. Commitment to truth imposed on him constant self-awareness and sincere self-analysis. It is this mindset that made Gandhi see *svarāja* simultaneously as political liberation and as self-rule in social, economic and spiritual realms. Romesh Thapar insightfully remarks on the subjective dimension:

> The quantum of untruth in you is the quantum of your failure to be true to yourself. This is one of the sublimated philosophical points in Hinduism which Gandhi absorbed. (67)

The uniqueness of Gandhian thought lies in its fusion of Upaniṣadic forbearance with activist insistence on the need to protect human rights.

Thus Gandhian non-violence is more than a philosophic precept. It is a way of life geared to the pursuit of values like truth and justice in a totally non-partisan frame of mind. It is also inter-linked with the ideals of self-discipline and selfless service. For a votary of non-violence, wilful causing of pain to others is anathema. The thrust of the Gandhian path is not on victory to the practitioner of non-violence but on victory of truth. As Hyder Ali Khan observes, when a victory is achieved through violence, ill-fellings in the heart of the defeated for ever remain. But when a non-violent fighter wins, he wins the heart of the foe (75). The Working Document of the UNESCO Symposium aptly highlights how

> non-violence opens the minds of men to freedom and disinterestedness allowing therefore a more sincere and objective recovery of a truth lost. (356-7)

The Gandhian goal is to win over opponents. It is now generally acknowledged that only such transformation can root out conflicts forever and replace the usual winner-loser animosity with mutual trust and respect.

When the choice for non-violence is made from a position of strength, that is, when people refrain from retaliation on moral grounds, and not out of cowardice or helplessness it cannot but create a new climate of sympathy and love in the world. The fasts that Gandhi used to undertake are not emotional blackmails but devout religious exercises undertaken for self-purification as part of the spiritual training enjoined by Hindu philosophy under the names *sāma*, *dāma* and *titīkṣā*.

Gandhi's greatness lies in stressing the need of non-violence not only in politics but also in day-to-day life. In the hands of Gandhi, *satyāgraha* was, indeed, to use the words of Prof. K.R Srinivas Iyengar, "the dynamic of moral action sustained by faith in God". (256) Gandhi tried to use it to revamp every sphere of life — politics, economics, education, administration and rural reconstruction — to establish what he loved to call a *sarvodaya* society — classless, casteless, nurtured not on the crass materiality of technological progress but on sloth-dispelling spiritual values like hard work, plain living and striving for the collective good of all members of the community rather than for individual prosperity. The best way to achieve socialism, according to Gandhi, is for everyone to use his or her property as a trustee for the benefit of fellow human beings.

It should be remembered that faith in non-violence has made Gandhi a man of action, not an armchair philosopher. The many institutions founded by him like the Phoenix Settlement near Durban, the Tolstoy Farm near Johannesburg, the Sabarmati Ashram at Wardha, together with his untiring efforts to restore peace during the trying time of communal riots, like those that broke out at Naokhali, show that all his life he had been a man of action and that he used non-violence as a magic charm to awaken the spark of divinity lying dormant in human hearts.

The mass movements Gandhi led are quite well known. Inspired by his example, innumerable non-violent campaigns were conducted in the far corners of India by Gandhi's followers: in Vykom of Kerala, for instance *satyāgrahī*s, braving police lathis, standing in the monsoon in shoulder deep water, maintained a sixteen-month resistance and secured for the so-called untouchables access to the temple road. In the district of Kotgarh, north of Simla, a custom approximating to temporary bonded labour was prevalent. For a nominal fee any passing

European official could secure the services of any number of farmers and enjoy the fruits of their labour. S.E. Stokes, an American, successfully led the non-violent struggle of the villagers for many months to end this exploitation.

No account of Gandhian non-violence can be complete without reference to the salt *satyāgraha*. The American Correspondent Webb Miller's despatch for the *New York Telegram*, dated 22 May 1930, offers a vivid eyewitness account of the incredible moral strength of thousands of unsung heroes.

> The scene at Dharsana during the raid was astonishing and baffling to the Western Mind accustomed to see violence met by violence. During the morning I saw and heard hundreds of blows inflicted by the police, but saw not a single blow returned by the volunteers. So far as I could observe, the volunteers implicitly obeyed Gandhi's creed of non-violence. In no case did I see a volunteer even raise an arm to deflect the blows from the lathis. There were no outcries from the beaten Swarajists, only groans after they had submitted to their beating. (Gregg, 16)

Impressed by Gandhi's personal charisma, Mountbatten hailed him as a 'one-man boundary force'. The simplicity of Gandhi's bearing and the vitality of his thought, the galvanising power of the Hindu traditions he imbibed and the universal applicability and relevance of his ideals are thoroughly integrated in the perceptive comment of the distinguished sociologists, Rudolph and Rudolph:

> In pursuing . . . transformations of Indian character, society and politics he used traditional symbols and language to convey new meanings and to reconstitute social action. Gandhi firmly believed that a person's capacity for Self-control enhanced his capacity to control his environment. This was the key to Gandhi's political potency. (Preface, viii)

The unfortunate proliferation of violence in India during the last two decades, the increase in both terrorist activities and police atrocities, the mounting crime rate, the rampant corruption in public life, the growing indiscipline in academies and the cropping-up of decadent trends in society like alcoholism and drug-addiction point to the sad truth that Indians have drifted away from Gandhian ideals and the perennial values embodied in them.

It is time we realise that Gandhian *dharma* is not a conglomerate of codes. Rather, it is a dynamic living principle dedicated to bring out the best in man and through that the best in the society around. Gandhian non-violence gives an opportunity to everyone to see the 'human dimension' in issues and thereby act as an automatic corrective to malice and hatred, the usual sources of enmity and discord.

Thus, Gandhian non-violence, based on the Vedāntic concept of one Reality pervading the inner and the outer worlds, and its implementation through and for spiritual regeneration, can bring about the much needed synergy of religion and science, ethics and economy and progress and peace.

References

Gandhi, M.K., *An Autobiography or The Story of My Experiments with Truth*, Mahadev Desai, tr., Navajivan Publishing House, 1927, Ahmedabad, 1959.

Gregg, Richard, B., *The Power of Non-violence*, Navajivan Publishing House, Ahmedabad, 1938, 1960.

Khan, Hyder Ali, *The Relevance of Mahatma Gandhi to the World of Thought*, Gandhi Centenary Volume, T.M.P. Mahadevan (ed.), University of Madras, Madras 1969, 73-9.

Radhakrishnan, S., *The Principal Upaniṣads*, George Allen and Unwin, London, 1953.

Raghavan, V., 'Traditional Roots of Some Leading Gandhian Ideas and Ideals' in Dr. T.M.P. Mahadevan (ed.), *The Relevance of Mahatma Gandhi to World Thought*, University of Madras, Madras, 1969, pp. 112-25.

Romulo, Carlos, Symposium paper, Report of the UNESCO Symposium on Truth and Non-violence in Gandhi's Humanism, T.K. Mahadevan (ed.), Gandhi Peace Foundation, New Delhi, 1970, pp. 317-25.

Rudolph Susanne, H. and Lloyd I. Rudolph, *Gandhi: The Tradition and Roots of Charisma*, Orient Longman, Hyderabad, 1987.

Srinivas Iyengar, K.R., *Indian Writing in English*, Sterling Publications, New Delhi, 1962, 1987.

Thapar, Romesh, Report of the UNESCO Symposium on *Truth and Non-violence in Gandhi*'s *Humanism*, T.K. Mahadevan (ed.), Gandhi Peace Foundation, New Delhi, 1970, Passim.

10

Swami Bala Siva Yogi

Spiritual Equality

K.R. Rajani

An attempt is made here to understand the ideas on social equality, spiritual equality, concept of love and self-consciousness expressed by Swami Bala Siva Yogendra Maharaj in different addresses and articles. Swami Bala Siva Yogendra Maharaj was born on 27 July 1954 to the devout couple, Smt. Thota Venkata Lakshmamma and Sri Rosaiah. As a child he was named as Eswara Vara Prasad. The most important turning point in Swamiji's life, is the day he had the transcendental experience of a huge ball of bright light approaching him and merging in him. Thereafter Swamiji was in a sealed room for 42 days without food and water, from 21 January 1973 to 3 March 1973, at Duvvur, 30 miles away from Cuddapah in Andhra Pradesh. Thus the young Hindu spiritual leader was born.

Swamiji's new and bold ideas on social order and equality are certainly a welcoming thought as contemporary India is still without any considerable social equality.

In the Golden Jubilee Celebrations of our Independence Day, on 15 August 1996, Dr. Sankar Dayal Sharma, the then President of India, appealed to us to strive for social equality. It is strange that, with all the treasure of classical thought and excellent traditions, India with its 54 years of independence unable to attain the fundamental character of social equality Now the question that arises here is, is it owing to our tradition or our interpretation of our tradition? The first question may be invalid on the ground that, the Vedas, which are the bedrock of our tradition, never speak of social inequality in any manner. But after the emergence of the Smṛtis, the caste system, which is the root cause of today's social inequality, gained importance perhaps in order to address some of the problems of that society. Then where is the ship of the Indian society anchored? Is it at the shore of peace to live harmoniously or that of social disorder arising from the war of castes? To give some effective solutions to this problem is the need of the day.

At this juncture Swami Bala Siva Yogindra Maharaj reflected upon this problem as a responsible living Hindu *guru*. Swamiji is really the successor of Vivekananda to the Parliament of World's Religions held in August-September, 1993. His presentation was "a great event, full of significance as was the Parliament of Religions in September, 1893".[1]

In his address Swamiji gave maximum stress on the theme of 'social equality'. Swamiji says that we must get rid of our weaknesses and "come out of *Manu-Smṛti*" for establishing a stable path of societal growth and to the basic spirituality of Hindu *dharma* for realising humanity as one family. Equality and fraternity can be firmly established in the human family only through the evolution of self-consciousness and realisation of equality of all *jīvātmā*s (souls). Peace among men and peace between man and nature have no meaning without this spiritual realisation of equality and fraternity.[2]

The realisation of the equality of the self, mind and body is possible through self-consciousness; thereby peace can be restored in true sense. In the same address, his (Swamiji's) lucid explanation of spirituality, which is the essence to realise the self-consciousness, has four hall-marks:[3]

(i) freedom of mind,
(ii) spiritual equality of souls,
(iii) bond of love as a motivating force in life, and
(iv) spirit of sacrifice.

To realise these four aspects in life one must feel and have equality of body, mind and soul not only with the 'Absolute' but also with every human being. This sense of oneness can never be realised unless we strive for spirituality as is emphatically said by Swamiji,

> The time has come for humanity to grow out of the organised religions and embrace spirituality which is the essence of all religions.[4]

Without spirit religion is of no use. The spirit alone leads to attain oneness and equality of all human beings. This perspective should be reinterpreted rightly with the help of traditional classics by the saints and scholars and should be propagated among masses in order to heraled social equality and a casteless Indian society.

Equality (oneness) of soul in Vedānta

The Upaniṣads or Vedānta have a considerable influence on the minds of the saints, seers and *gurus* of contemporary India and Swamiji is no exception to this. The *Bṛhadāraṇyaka Upaniṣad*, chapter IV, section V, verse 7 says:[5]

> The *Brahman* ousts (slights) one who knows him as different from the Self. The Kshatriya ousts one who knows him as different from the Self. Worlds oust one who knows them as different from the Self. The gods oust one who knows them as different from the Self. The Vedas oust one who knows them as different from the Self. Beings oust one who knows them as different from the Self. All ousts one who knows it as different from the Self. This Brahmana, this Kshatriya, these worlds, these gods, these *Veda*s, these beings and this all — are this Self.

Again the *Bṛhadāraṇyaka Upaniṣad*, chapter II, section IV, verses 7 to 10, says thus:

> As, when a drum is beaten, one cannot distinguish its various particular notes, but they are included in the

general note of the drum or in the general sound produced by different kinds of strokes.

As when, a conch is blown, one cannot distinguish its various particular notes, but they are included in the general note of the conch or in the general sound produced by different kinds of playing.

As, when a *vīnā* is played, one cannot distinguish its various particular notes, but they are included in the general note of the *vīnā* or in the general sound produced by different kinds of playing.

As from a fire kindled with wet faggot diverse kinds of smoke issue, even so, my dear, the *Ṛgveda*, *Yajurveda*, *Sāmaveda*, *Atharvangirasa*, *history*, *mythology*, *arts*, *Upaniṣads*, *Pithy verses*, *Aphorisms*, elucidations and explanations are (like) the breath of this infinite Reality. They are like the breath of this (Supreme Self).

The same Upaniṣad, chapter II, section V, verse 1 says:

This earth is (like) honey (effect or helpful) to all beings, and all beings are (like) honey to this earth. (The same with) the shining immortal being who is in this earth, and the shining, immortal, corporeal being in the body (these four) are but this Self. This (self-knowledge is the means of) immortality; this (underlying unity) is *Brahman*; this (knowledge of *Brahman*) is (the means of becoming) all.

In the *Taittirīya Upaniṣad*, III Vallī, 2-6, Bhṛgu analyses the five phases of Brahmā as follows:[6]

Having performed austerity, he understood
that *Brahman* is food. For truly, indeed,
beings here are born from food, when born, they live by food, on decease they enter into food.

Like this, the '*kośa* theory' states that *anna*, *prāṇa*, *manas*, *vijñāna* and *ānanda* are *Brahman*, the Self and advocates the equality of self. The *Īśa Upaniṣad*, verse 7 says:

> In whom all beings
> Have become just (*eva*) the Self of the discerner.
> Then what delusion (*moha*), what sorrow (*śoka*) is
> there of him who perceives the unity.

The *Śvetāśvatara Upaniṣad*, IV, verse 10, says:

> Now, one should know that nature (*prakṛti*) is illusion
> (*māyā*)
> And the Mighty Lord (*maheśvara*) is the illusion
> maker (*māyin*)
> This whole world is pervaded
> With beings that are parts of Him.

A clear understanding, of the above Upaniṣadic passages, reveals that there is only one reality, which becomes many. When everyone becomes known as one with the knower, there is no question of grief for the person who sees oneness or equality everywhere. This realisation of spiritual equality is the way of salvation. In this precarious situation of Indian society today, every Indian and not seers and *guru*s alone, must commit themselves to the task of restoring social and spiritual equality to attain peace.

Reference

1. Swami Bala Siva Yogindra Maharaj presented a paper 'Hinduism and Concept of God' on 3 September, 1993, in the Second Parliament of World's Religions, 1993, Chicago. Vide: M. Gopalakrishna Reddy, *Second Parliament of World's Religions 1993, Chicago Addresses of Swami Bala Siva Yogendra Maharaj*, p. 1.
2. *Ibid.*, pp. 12-13.
3. *Second Parliament of World's Religions 1993, Chicago Addresses of Swami Bala Siva Yogendra Maharaj*, p. 9.
4. *Ibid.*
5. All the following quotations are from Swami Madhavananda, tr.,

Bṛhadāraṇyaka Upaniṣad with the Commentary of Śaṅkarācārya, 4th edn., 1965.

6. All the following quotations are from Robert Earnest Hume, *The Thirteen Principal Upaniṣads*, 1954, pp. 290-1.

11

Mahatma Gandhi
A Secular Saint

G.S.R. Raju

RELIGION played a dominant role in all ancient cultures especially in India, where it was the prime factor moulding the lives of the people for ages. Religion enables a man to control and regulate his lower self of desires by the law of the higher self. Religion places before man the ideals of perfection and provides the inner urge to move towards it. It is a part of the nature of man to aspire and to transcend his finiteness and become one with the Absolute or God.

Religion is not magic or witchcraft, quackery or superstition. It is not to be confused with the outdated dogmas and incredible superstitions which are hindrances and barriers that spoil the simplicity of spiritual life. Indeed the practice of the scientific philosophy of *Yoga Sūtras* of Patañjali has been universally recognised as an essential prerequisite to maintain sound mental and physical health in any man.

God and truth

Gandhi's religion is a rational and ethical one. For, he does not accept any belief which does not appeal to his reason and which does not commend itself to his conscience. Herein, we are confronted with the problem: What is Gandhi's religion? And how his religion is rational and ethical? Gandhi's fundamental religious presupposition is — 'God is Truth'.[1] According to Gandhi, "God can be found only through love, not earthly, but divine".[2]

And Gandhi's rational pre-supposition is — 'Truth is God'.[3] It is further stated that "his uniform experience has convinced him that there is no other God than truth".[4]

It is important to note about Gandhi's conviction that for him truth is the sovereign principle. This truth is not only truthfulness in word and thought, and not only the relative truth of our conception, but the absolute truth, the eternal principle, God. Hence, Gandhi said,

> I worship God as truth only. I have not yet found Him, but I am seeking after Him. I am prepared to sacrifice the things dearest to me in pursuit of this quest. But as long as I have not realised this absolute truth, so long must I hold by the relative truth as I have conceived it. Meanwhile, that relative truth must be my beacon, my shield and buckler . . . I have kept strictly to this path.[5]

It is with this conviction that Gandhi declared that his life was an experiment with truth. As such, it is obvious that for Gandhi a religion that did not concern itself with every side of life was no religion at all. Thus, the foundation of Gandhi's life was formed by his living and growing faith in God and in the oneness of the whole human family. According to Gandhi, the discipline, which every man should follow, is non-violence in order to realise the highest ideals, whether we call it God, or truth, or humanity, and it is common to all.

Morality in religion

Gandhi stated,

> I reject any religious doctrine that does not appeal to reason and is in conflict with morality. I tolerate unreasonable religious sentiment when it is not immoral.[6]

Herein, Gandhi also expressed his conviction that as soon as we lose the moral basis, we cease to be religious. There is no such thing as religion overriding morality. For instance, man being untruthful, cruel and incontinent cannot claim to have God on his side. For Gandhi, religion which takes no account of practical affairs and does not help to solve them is no religion.

Thus Gandhi was rational enough to make it clear about his fundamental religious approach that he considered anything which was against morality as irrational and not religion at all. Then, Gandhi logically deduced his another fundamental moral pre-supposition:

> Non-violence is soul-force or the power of God-head within us. We become God-like to the extent we realise non-violence.[7]

Hence, it implies that one becomes truthful to the extent he follows non-violence. That is why, Gandhi further states that

> when you want to find truth as God the only inevitable means is Love, i.e. non-violence.[8]

That is why, it was through this conviction of non-violence that throughout his life Gandhi firmly and persistently resisted evil or injustice in any walk of life, in any society through the means of non-violence. As a practical idealist Gandhi exposed and advocated that the religion of non-violence was not meant for the *ṛṣis* and saints. It was meant for the common people as well, and also for the nations of the world.

Means and Ends

Gandhi's firm conviction was that

> without *Ahimsa* (non-violence) it is not possible to seek and find truth. *Ahimsa* is the means, and truth is the end. Means to be means must always be within our reach, and so *Ahimsa* is our supreme duty. If we take care of the means, we are bound to reach the end sooner or later.[9]

It is important to note Gandhi's faith in non-violence and truth. Gandhi stated that his love for non-violence was superior to every other thing mundane or supermundane. It was equalled only by his love for truth, which was synonymous with non-violence through which and which alone one could see and reach truth. Hence, it is obvious that Gandhi insisted to bring ethical values to regulate social, political and economic fields of human activity from which spheres the essential moral values had been absent. So, here in the present age of moral degeneration and in the midst of the tribulations of a distracted world, Gandhi is message of truth and non-violence bear special relavance.

As a matter of fact, when Gandhi talks of spiritualising politics, he only means making politics moral. What is sought to be introduced into politics in India by Gandhi is the standard of ethical and honourable conduct, whether in individual life or in political life.

Politics and morality

The inspiration of Gandhi's life has been what is commonly called religion. Religion for Gandhi is not in the sense of subscription to dogmas or conformity to ritual, but religion is an abiding faith in the absolute values of truth, non-violence and justice and a persistent endeavour to realise them on earth. Gandhi drafted a code of vows for the observance of the members of his ashrama.

1. Vow of truth
2. Vow of *ahiṁsā* (non-violence)
3. Vow of *brahmacarya* (celibacy)
4. Vow of control of the palate
5. Vow of non-stealing
6. Vow of non-possession or poverty
7. Vow of *svadeśī*
8. Vow of fearlessness
9. Vow regarding the untouchables
10. Vow of *khādī*
11. Vow of education through the vernacular
12. Vow of the religious use of politics

The desire for spiritual perfection is rooted in the very nature of man. Such aspiration works consciously or sub-consciously within him. According to Gandhi, realisation of 'Truth or God' is the ultimate goal of human race. Therefore, man's life is to undergo certain ethical and spiritual discipline for achieving that end. To him, discipline regarding non-violence, celibacy, non-possession, fearlessness, removal of social prejudices, bread-labour, *svadeśī*, and equality of all religions constitute the very structure of *satyāgraha* or truth force or soul force. *Satyāgraha* or soul force is the perfect weapon to win political freedom as to attain spiritual destiny.

Ethical philosophy

Gandhi has been called a 'moral revolutionary' and also a 'moral genius'. To him, morality is the basic principle of life. He endeavours to establish '*Rāmarājya*' or the 'Kingdom of God' in our country through certain rigid moral disciplines. Gandhi declares that for political and social betterment of mankind, moral regeneration is essential. Moral growth controls passions and impulses of man which lead to violence, strife and destruction, and urges him to work for peace, harmony and happiness. In fact, the sense of morality or the conscience of man is his inner guide to lead him to a higher destiny.

Human beings can achieve moral ideals only by a gradual process, which requires thinking capacity, proper consideration and a very strong will. Gandhi admits it and says,

> The ideals that regulate my life are presented for acceptance by mankind in general. I have arrived at them by gradual evolution. Every step was thought out, well considered and taken with the greatest deliberation.[10]

Human desires and motives can be divided into two classes — selfish and unselfish. Selfish desires are immoral. The desire to do good for others improves the doer's nature and that service is considered to be truly moral. Moral force originates from the determination

> to do something, to sacrifice something for the sake of humanity. Therefore, the moral greatness of a person

> can be measured only by his benevolent service towards humanity.

Gandhi stated that

> Man becomes great exactly in the degree in which he works for the welfare of his fellow men.[11]

Gandhi prescribes certain moral principles for the development of man's ethical personality. These principles are correlated and are recognised by most of the great religions of the world. Such principles clearly reveal that Gandhi "found for humanity a civilised way for righting wrongs and establishing justice". These principles are: (a) non-violence, (b) *brahmacarya*, (c) non-possession, (d) fearlessness, and (e) self-purification. Apart from discipline to ensure practise of *ahiṁsa* and other vows, mentioned above, he also favours certain other devices for the purification of the human soul. They include feeling for humanity, fasting and maintaining silence.

According to Gandhi, self-purification means "purification in all the walks of life". He further says that to attain perfect purity one has to become absolutely passion-free in thought, speech and action; and one has to rise above the opposing currents of love and hatred, attachment and repulsion. He considers the desireless service (*niṣkāma karma*) as the best worship. It can be performed only when man's soul is fully purified. He was greatly fascinated by the *Gītā*'s conception of *yajña*, sacrifice. For him, without *yajña*, the world cannot submit even for a brief while. He points out,

> *Yajñā* means an act directed to the welfare of others, done without desiring any return for it, whether of a temporal or spiritual nature.[12]

Gandhi says that man's religious nature should be closely related with his moral life, because religion without morality has no meaning. To an ethical person, "ethics and religion are convertible terms".[13] Man who loses his moral bias, cannot claim himself to be religious. Gandhi has no sympathy for a religious doctrine which does not appeal to reason and which is not associated with morality. Again religion, which does not help man to solve the problems of his practical life, cannot be regarded as true religion. He declares that no man can live without religion. There are some, who in the egotism of their reason, declare that they have nothing to do with religion. But it is like a man saying that he breathes but that he has no nose. Whether by reason or by instinct, or by superstition, man acknowledges some sort of relationship with the divine.

Destiny of man

Gandhi holds that the imperfect man can become perfect by the complete realisation of Truth, which is the other name of God. The realisation of truth is regarded by Gandhi as man's final destiny. According to him, "To find truth completely is to realise oneself and one's destiny i.e., to become perfect".[14] Hence, it is the duty of every man to become a relentless seeker after truth. As a true guide of humanity, Gandhi evolves and emphasises many ethical and spiritual ways by which man can reach his destined goal. *Satyāgraha*, *ahiṁsā*, truth, faith or intuition are the principal ways of Gandhi for the attainment of the long-cherished destiny of mankind. In his *Gandhian Ethics*, B.G. Ray says,

> that which is illogical and immoral was always repugnant to him. The Vedas, Upanishads, Gita and Puranas were acceptable to Gandhi provided they appealed to his reason.[15]

Gandhi is a man of practical outlook. Whatever he has said and written has been meant only to solve the practical problems of mankind. What Gandhi wants to do is to exalt the human race from the narrow boundaries of life to the highest ethical plane. For this purpose, Gandhi has discovered the principle of *satyāgraha* basing it on non-violence. Referring to the novelty and the greatness of the principle of *satyāgraha*, Einstein writes,

> Gandhi has invented an entirely new and human technique for the liberation struggle of an oppressed

> people and carried it out with the greatest energy and devotion.[16]

Any elderly man who has seen life before India's independence is appalled to find the degeneration that has set in today. This process of moral degeneration started in the early periods of independent India which compelled Radhakrishnan to say that,

> We live in an age which is aware of its own defeat and moral coarsening, and in which old certainties are breaking down, the familiar patterns are tilting and cracking. There is increasing intolerance and embitterment. The creative flame that kindled the great human society is languishing. It is our pride that one of the greatest figures of history lived in our generation.

Gandhi's ideology of non-violence and truth transcended the bounds of his country and people. He became not only the liberator of his motherland from the yoke of alien rule and of his people from social evils but also the leader of mankind as a whole. We call him not only the 'Father of the Nation' but also the greatest man the world has seen for many a century. Gandhi was a son of India but a citizen of the whole world. On Gandhi's death on 30 January 1948, Jawaharlal Nehru said,

> The Light has gone out of our lives, it was no ordinary Light. The Light that has illumined this country for these many years will illumine this country for many more years and a thousand years later that Light will still be seen in this country and the world will see it and it will give solace to innumerable hearts. For that Light represented the living Truth.

Reference

1. M.K. Gandhi, *My Religion*, Navajeevan, 1955, p. 30.
2. M.K. Gandhi, *Satyagraha in South Africa*, p. 237.
3. M.K. Gandhi, *My Religion*, p. 39.
4. M.K. Gandhi, *An Autobiography*, vol. II, p. 752.

5. M.K. Gandhi, *My Religion*, p. 41.
6. M.K. Gandhi, *Young India*, 21-7-1920.
7. M.K. Gandhi, *Harijan*, 12-11-1938, p. 326.
8. M.K. Gandhi, *My Religion*, p. 40.
9. M.K. Gandhi, *Form Yarvada Mandir*, pp. 12-13.
10. M.K. Gandhi, *Young India*, 20-2-1930, p. 61.
11. M.K. Gandhi, *The Art of Living*, p. 63.
12. Ronald Duncan, ed., *Selected Writings of Mahatma Gandhi*, p. 16.
13. M.K. Gandhi, *My Religion*, p. 3.
14. M.K. Gandhi, *Truth is God*, p. 3.
15. Mahadeva Prasad, *Social Philosophy of Mahatma Gandhi*, p. 5.
16. A. Einstein, '*Gandhi*'s *Statesmanship*', in *Essays and Reflections on His Life and Work*, S. Radhakrishnan (ed.), p. 74.

12

Sri Shirdi Sai Baba
His Life and Message

S. Satyanarayana

SRI Shirdi Sai Baba is known in almost all parts of our country and abroad and has many devotees all over the world. People after seeing His love for humanity and the utmost importance accorded by Him to all creatures in nature have become the followers or *bhaktas*. His only aim is to reduce the problems of the humanity. Whosoever comes to Him gets solace automatically. All of his followers consider Him as the most powerful and popular God or *bhagavān* or *avatāra-puruṣa* and the *avatāra* of modern times.

According to His devotees, Shirdi Sai is the incarnation of Lord Śīva. Some of His followers believed. He was another *avatāra* of Sri guru Dattatreya. Even some Muslim brothers express that their God Allāh came once again in the form of Shirdi Sai. In this way, except a few, almost all consider Him as a godly person who came down from heaven to earth to protect *dharma* and *satya* and to lead humanity as a whole towards divinity. His *avatāra* is very much in tune with the following *śloka* of the *Bhagavad Gītā*:

> *yadā-yadā hi dharmasya, glānir bhavati bhārata*
> *abhyutthānamadharmasya, tad-ātmanam sr̥jāmyaham.*
> *paritrāṇāya sādhūnām, vināśāya ca duṣkr̥tām,*
> *dharma saṁsthāpanārthhāya, sambhavāmi yuge-yuge.*

> Whenever there is decay of righteousness, O Bharata, and rise of unrighteousness, then I manifest myself. For the protection of the Good and the destruction of the wicked and for the establishment of righteousness I am born in every age.[1]

Brief life sketch

There are different opinions and sometimes controversies about the life story of Sri Shirdi Sai Baba. He never mentioned His birthplace clearly to any of His devotees. Many devotees tried to know about His family background. But they failed because whenever they asked Sai about it, He just smiled at them and did not tell them anything. During His conversations with His *bhakta*s He might have told a few words but they could not formulate a full life story of Sai. But his followers formulated a brief account based on the few words said by Sai. This tells us about the life history of Shirdi Sai. He was born in a pious brāhmaṇa family and unfortunately under unavoidable circumstances He was left in the forest on their journey to divinity. He was then brought up by a Muslim as a child given by Allāh. Due to social and religious sentiments, the Muslim was told to leave this Bala Sai in the forest and pressure to this effect came upon him from the Hindus and the Muslims. Due to all this, the Muslim died after some time. The wife of the Muslim took care of the child and at the age of 12 years He was sent to an *āśrama* for educational training under the guidance of *sadguru* Venkusa.

Under His *guru* Bala Sai learned strict discipline and the things needed for real life. His *guru* was very much pleased with His devotion and dedication for work. That is why He was very much liked by his *guru*. Some students in the ashrama did not like this. He faced a lot of problems there also. He could not adjust with the atmosphere of the ashrama. So He was almost compelled to leave the place after getting permission from his *guru*.

From the ashrama Bala Sai reached a small village, Shirdi exactly at the age of 16 and meditated under a neem tree in *padmāsana*. He tolerated all seasons under the neem tree and never tilted from the position assumed during meditation. He never opened His mouth to talk with the people around. He attracted many people because of His *tapas-śakti*. And people saw Aroma and wanted to talk with Him but He never allowed them to talk with him. People were waiting for a chance. Those were the days when the famous festival of Devī Khāṇḍobā was celebrated with great pomp like our *Daśahara* festival today.

During that festival Goddess Khāṇḍobā entered the body of a person there. Then the people of the village asked him about Bala Sai. Then the person told them to dig deep under the neem tree. They did as guided by the Devī Khāṇḍobā. There they found a way into earth and discovered *pūjā sāmagrī* and four lighted candles. Then the Khāṇḍobhā Devī also told them that Bala Sai had gained many spiritual powers. Then, Bala Sai opened His mouth and requested the people to close down the place digged. This was the first occasion when Bala Sai talked with the people. From that time onwards people started coming to Him and this disturbed His meditation. For this reason, Bala Sai left this place in search of truth and propagation of peace.

During this period, a Fakir Sab came to the surrounding places of the village, Auraṅgābād where He met Chand Patel and helped him to get his lost horse and showed them His miracles. Chand Patel recognised the Fakir Sab as a divine person and requested Him to visit His house once. Fakir Sab visited the house of Chand Patel and became very close to Him and Chand Patel became the first devotee of Fakir Sab. From this time onwards, Fakir Sab used to visit Chand Patel and stayed there for a few days whenever He visited him.

With this intimacy one day Chand Patel requested Fakir Sab to attend his relative's marriage to be held at Shirdi village. So Fakir Sab along with his friend Chand Patel went to Shirdi to attend the marriage. All went there in a bullock cart. After reaching the village all of them stopped under a banyan tree very near to the temple of Goddess Khāṇḍobā. One by one, all the members got down from the bullock cart. While Fakir Sab was getting down from the bullock cart the *pujārī* of the temple, Mahalasapati, recognised Fakir Sab as Bala Sai who had disappeared from Shirdi long back and with ecstasy and tears rolling down his eyes, Mahalasapati welcomed the Fakir Sab *āiye sāī* (Please come, Swāmī). ('Sai' means Swami in Marāṭhī).

From that day onwards, the name 'Sai' became permanently associated with Him. Sai made a very ancient mosque as his residence and lived there until *samādhi*. Even after *samādhi*, Sai devotees believe that 'He is still alive'. The devotees get whatever they want from the *samādhi*. So, Sai is *ciranjīvī* and blesses his *bhakta*s in the same way as He did when He lived in human form.

Main Teachings of Sri Shirdi Sai Baba

The teachings of Shirdi Sai Baba are very simple. All His teachings tell us how to live happily with the help of a *sadguru*, how to love each other and how to reach the Almighty at the end. He believes that all religions are same and meant for the happiness of man. Some views of Shirdi Sai Baba are given here:[2]

- There are many ways of God realisation or divine experience. There is one way from Shirdi too.
- The realisation of God or the divine experience is very difficult without a perfect *sadguru* because there are wild animals in the jungles on the way. If we take the help of a *sadguru*, then there will be no difficulty because the *sadguru* will show the way, avoiding all the wild animals in the jungles.
- Do your duty, don't be afraid in the least. Steady your mind and have complete faith in my words.
- Meditation is necessary for Self-realisation to get the experience of God.
- If we practise meditation continuously, every thought will be pacified. Being quiet and desireless, you should

meditate on the Lord. When the mind is concentrated, the goal will be achieved.

- Meditate always on 'Me', the formless nature, that is knowledge, consciousness and bliss.
- If you cannot do this, meditate on my form from top to toe as you see me here day and night. As you go on doing this, your thoughts will not be pointed and the difference between the mediator, the object of meditation and the things to be meditated upon will disappear and the mediator will be merged in the *Brahman* — united and becoming one with the consciousness.
- If you always say 'Sai Sai' I shall take you over the seven seas. Believe in these words and you will be certainly benefited.
- Love and belief only are important to me. Where there is pure devotion and love I rest there only. Where real love and devotion exist, that is my real residence.
- If any body utters my name with love, I shall fulfil his wishes and increase his devotion.
- Those devotees who are attached to 'Me' with their heart and soul, will naturally feel happiness. When they hear my stories, believe me, I will certainly protect them from all troubles. If any body sings my *līlā*s, I will give him infinite joy and everlasting contentment.
- It is my special characteristic to free any person who surrenders completely to 'Me' and who does worship 'Me' faithfully and who remembers 'Me' faithfully and meditates on 'Me' constantly.
- Be wherever you like, do whatever you choose, remember this well that what you do is known to me.
- I am the inner ruler of all and seated in their hearts.
- I only create all the creatures of the nature and I am the controller of the universe.

- Pāṇḍuraṅga Viṭṭhala is here. Dvārakā of Śrī Kṛṣṇa is here. Ayodhayāvāsī Śrī Rāma is here, Yesu Prabhu is here, Allāh is here. Everything is here. One need not go far to see them.

- The force of *karma* is driven here and so I asked that amount from him as *dakṣiṇā*.

- Debt, enemity and murders must be atoned for, as there is no escape from these.

- If I take one rupee as *dakṣiṇā* from anybody I have to return in tenfold to him.

- Wealth should be a the means to do *dāna* and *dharma*. If it is used completely for personal enjoyment, it will be a waste completely — whatever wealth you have. You should use it for *dharma* and *dāna*.

- Unless you have given it before, you do not get it now. So the best way to receive is to give.

- The Lord of all beings is One and same: *sabkā mālik ek*.

- Except your name and form something is there inside of you. That is 'Me', that is the life energies. That is *ātman*. That is present in all the living beings and that is 'Me'.

- I am neither God nor Love. I am his obedient servant and remember him always.

- He who keeps his egoism aside and thinks of Him always and he who trusts Him completely will have his burdens and problems solved and will obtain liberation or *mokṣa*.

- Allāh will take care of you. Think of Allāh always. Allāh is the sole protector.

- I feel always anxiety for the betterment of my devotees.

- Let us do our prescribed duty and surrender our body, mind and five *prāṇa*s at *sadguru*'s feet. *Guru* is God, *guru* is all-pervading. To get this conviction, strong and unbounded faith is needed.

- Keep always your faith on any one God in one place. No use by roaming on to that God or this God or this place or that place. Slick quietly to one place that you like and keep your faith in that one place.
- I have no form, nor any extension. So I require no door to enter.
- If you want to do anything to others, do good only.
- Never refuse offered food.
- Make 'Me' as the sole object of your thoughts and actions and you no doubt can attain *paramātmā*.
- Have faith and confidence in your *guru*, that the *sadguru* is the sole doer and actor.
- Blessed is he who knows the greatness of his *sadguru* and thinks him as the real form of Brahmā, Viṣṇu and Maheśvara *svarūpa*.
- Pure Love is the perfect form of my *sadguru*.
- I always look to and provide for the welfare of those devotees who worship 'Me' wholeheartedly with their minds ever fixed on 'Me'.
- My bones will answer to the problems of my devotees even from my *samādhi*.
- I am ever living to help and guide who come to Me, who surrender to Me and who seek refuge in Me.
- If you look to Me I look to you.
- There shall be no want in the house of my devotees.
- If anybody believes me completely, no doubt I shall draw them out even from the jaws of death.
- I always look to and provide for the welfare of those devotees who worship *oṁ* wholeheartedly with their minds ever fixed on 'Me'.

- I shall be ever active and more vigorous even after leaving this earthly body.
- If you seek my advice and help, it shall be given to you at once at any time.
- My *samādhi* shall bless and speak to the needs of my devotees.
- Whoever puts his feet on Shirdi soil his sufferings would come to an end.
- Everyone including all religions and castes, the wretched and the miserable would rise into plenty of joy and happiness as soon as they enter the steps of my *samādhi* at Shirdi.
- I surely protect all my devotees at any time and anywhere.

Reference

1. Swami Chinmayananda, *The Bhagavad Gītā*, pp. 384-5.
2. I have taken some of these teachings of Sai from the book entitled *The Sayings of Shirdi Sai* by Agastya Raju Ravindra.

13

Sri Chandrasekharendra Saraswati

The Sage of Kāñcī

V.N. Seshagiri Rao

AT the outset, I submit that it is difficult to write about the saints and sages. They are dimensions of eternity and spiritual geniuses of the human race. They embody all good things. They look upon all as equal. Hence their teachings are too deep to delve into. But this does not mean that we should be ignorant of their magnificent acts and accomplishments. Prof. T.M.P. Mahadevan beautifully puts it:

> Meditation on the lives of the saints and on their teachings is a potent means to elevating our own lives and for gaining sublimity.[1]

Sri Chandrasekharendra Saraswati was the sixty-eighth *ācārya* in the hallowed line of succession of Śaṅkarācāryas to adorn the Kāmakoṭi Pīṭha of Kāñcī. He was a unique person of rare qualities and a remarkable character. He was free from passions like hate and fear. He possessed all the essentials of saintliness and sainthood. Kāñcī, the famous city of crowning temples, was the centre of his spiritual enlightenment. From times immemorial Kāñcī has been regarded as one of the *mokṣapurīs* of India. Śaṅkara, the famous and influential teacher of Advaita Vedānta, had intimate connections with this city. He is supposed to have consecrated Śrī Kāmākṣi and Śrī Cakra in Kāñcīpuram. He ascended the Sarvajñapīṭha at Kāñcī. Thus Kāñcī has been the centre of Kāmakoṭi Pīṭha. Sri Chandrasekharendra Saraswati lived there for more than a century and did intense penance (*tapas*) for the betterment of the whole world.

The sage of Kāñcī stands for the reinterpretation of Bhāratīya *vidyā*. It has been the content of a continuous process of interpretation right from the time of the Vedas up to the present day. The teachings, both oral and written, of Sri Chandrasekharendra Saraswati, reverentially called *paramācārya*, stimulate readers to be conscious of the renascent spirit of India. They ushered in a new era of intellectual, moral and spiritual development. True to the appellation as a *śiṣya vatsala*, he was known for taking a personal interest in the studies and requirements of the students. His lectures created in the minds of the readers a spirit of consecration removing psychological doubts and aspersions. He asked them to fervently adhere to the permanent values.

Sri Chandrasekharendra Saraswati is a *saṁnyāsa* name. In his *pūrvāśrama* his name was as Swamynathan. He was born on 20th May 1894 in Viluppuram, South Arcot district, Tamil Nadu; Subrahmanya Sastri was his father and his mother was Mahalakshmi. He was initiated into *saṁnyāsa* at the age of thirteen, in 1907. He ascended the Śrī Kāñcī Kāmakoṭi Pīṭha on 13-14 February 1907. He became the spiritual leader and was acclaimed as the *jagadguru*, the world teacher.

Paramācārya then took victory tours (*vijayayātra*) to different parts of the country to bless people, to perform worship for *loka-kalyāṇa* and to deliver discourses. He offered daily worship to Sri Chandramouli and Sri Tripura Sundari, the presiding deities of the Kāñcī Kāmakoṭi Pīṭha.

As a young *ācārya*, he took instructions in Sanskrit classics under the guidance of learned *paṇḍit*s of the *pīṭha*. He improved his knowledge of sciences and arts through elaborate discussions with the experts in the field. He acquired encyclopaedic knowledge of spiritual matters. Subrāhmaṇya Bhāratī, the renowned national poet, paid respects to the *paramācārya*. The *paramācārya* used to arrange *sada*s to enable all distinguished scholars to participate. He stood for the propagation of classical learning, arts and social service. People from all religions — Hinduism, Islam, Christianity — became his disciples. He arranged to run a Vedic *pāṭhaśālā*. Mahatma Gandhi also met him and sought his blessings. He took personal interest in the renovation of temples and their regular conduct of daily worship. He also visited the celebrated Madras Sanskrit College and received benedictions. He was received at Kāśī, under the leadership of Pundit Madan Mohan Malaviya. He stood for inter-religious faith and understanding.

The Śrī Kāñcī Kāmakoṭi Pīṭha thus is a spiritual centre of service and is exerting its utmost to spread Bhāratīya *vidyā*. Its objective is reinterpretation of the Hindu culture in the light of the universal teachings of Śaṅkara, the celebrated *vedāntin* and a great social reformer. The teachings of the sage of Kāñcī reveal the deeper implications and impulsions of Bhāratīya *vidyā*.

Paramācārya, it may be said, reflects the greatness of Ādi-Śaṅkara. The fundamental values of Hinduism find their pristine vigour in his teachings. What he has received in meditation has poured out in love for the benefit of the entire mankind. His lectures held audience spellbound. All newspapers, including *The Hindu*, considered it their sacred duty to report these lectures in great detail.

Let us now examine, in detail, the real import of the teachings of *paramācārya*. He thinks that Advaita is a ladder to universal perfection. He declares that the nature of reality is non-dual — that is *Brahman* or *ātman*. We, in essence, are that. There is no fundamental difference between the human soul and *Brahman*. *Brahman* is *sat*, *cit*, *ānanda*. It is pure consciousness (*śuddha caitanya*), infinite (*ananta*). It is never born and therefore never dies. It is birthless and deathless. It is indestructible (*avināśī*). It is eternal (*nitya*). It is here, it is there. It is Self-luminous (*svayam prakāśa*) and Self-established (*svayam siddha*). It is unchanging and unchangeable (*apariṇām*). It is free from all pain, thirst and hunger.

But what has really happened in empirical life? Due to ignorance, the human Self fails to know its own real nature.

Owing to superimposition (*adhyāsa*), man who is *Brahman* in essence wrongly identifies himself with the body and hence undergoes all sufferings. So Advaita Vedānta declares that all are of the nature of Īśvara. What we see in this world as many are illusory. The real aim of man is to come out of this suffering caused by the birth and death of the body (*śarīra*). The goal is called *mokṣa*, which consists in realising the eternal nature of the self. Thus for the destruction of misery, Advaita is the best medicine. Even in practical life, we see that if two minds become one, there is no strife.

Thus Advaita, according to *paramācārya*, is a grand discipline for the realisation of values. Values go to constitute Reality. Strictly speaking, though the ultimate Reality is *nirguṇa Brahman*, in popular parlance, it is called God. How to come out of the trials and tribulations of life? What is the way out? *Paramācārya* says, by submitting one's sweet will to the Lord. It is otherwise called *bhakti* or devotion. *Bhakti* is the essential foundation of the truly Vedāntic life. Man should seek God's grace through worship and meditation. The quality of life should be improved. The mind can be purified by undertaking meditation; and the purified mind becomes fit to discriminate between the real and the unreal, between the eternal and the non-eternal. This results in the down of knowledge. *Paramācārya* says that respect for *dharma* must be inculcated in the young minds. One may go without food or water, but not without daily discipline of divine worship. He showed this through example and precept. The blessings of God should be sought everyday. It is a must for enlightenment. The appropriate prayer to God, according to *paramācārya*, is to seek the happiness of all. The Upaniṣadic *mantra* best represents this:

sarva sukhinaḥ santu, sarve santu nirāmayaḥ,
sarve bhadrāṇi-paśyantu, mā kaścit duḥkha bhāg bhavet.

Let all be happy; let all be healthy; let all see the auspicious; let no one be miserable.

Paramācārya worked for a strong and resurgent Hinduism

and always had in his mind the betterment of the world. At all costs, ancient wisdom, that is *dharma,* should be preserved.

In the view of *paramācārya*, no man is wicked by nature, but circumstances compel him to be so. Upbringing also adds to the stock. One should not be impatient with the so-called wicked. Sympathy and compassion should be shown for them.

> Let me seek the same Self in the wicked man. Let me not hate him.[2]

According to *paramācārya*, religion is the way to inward peace. There is peace in unity and what leads to unity is religion. The *bījamantra* of Advaita as religion is *samanvaya* (harmony). It highlights and heralds the idea of the spirit of acceptance. It wholeheartedly welcomes and accepts what is regarded as truth in other religions. Acceptance is not because of fear or lack of knowledge; it is radical acceptance, knowing fully well the truth of other religions. And acceptance goes with rights. That is, all religions have equal rights and shares in truth. In other words, we should not be cynical of the salvation motive of different religions. *Paramācārya* discouraged the rivalries between different religions. He strongly pleaded for inter-religious understanding. He ardently advocated the coexistence of all religions. He held dear to his heart enlightened religiosity. Unity is the common idea that is found in all religions. All religions should get united in rejoicing over the idea of the supremacy of God. But why should there be different religions at all? *Paramācārya* says that the tastes of people are different (*loko bhinna rūciḥ*) and hence they follow different religions. But there should not be any room for religious fanaticism. Religions should strive for unity and not uniformity. Dispelling ignorance should be the main object of all religions. The teachings of *paramācārya* thus exalt and enable the lives of all people. For him, like Śaṅkara, the entire universe is a family, *vasudhaiva kuṭumbakam*.

Religion in the Hindu context is called *dharma*. And it is held in great reverence as it sustains society and the individual. *Paramācārya* regards *dharma* as a means to *mokṣa*, if it is followed without desiring fruit. *Dharma* is not only a duty but also a means to *mokṣa*. *Paramācārya* emphasises on duty. Without performing our duty, we cannot gain freedom from action. The aim is to attain a state of actionlessness by performing action. By doing so, we can become eligible to obtain God's grace, whereupon Supreme good is attained.

Advaita, thus, is the life mission of *paramācārya* as it was for Śaṅkara. It has no quarrel with any religion or faith. Everyone is included in its wide compass. Other religions may quarrel with Advaita; but in turn, Advaita does not quarrel with other religions. Sometimes, this stand of *paramācārya* on God is criticised. In Advaita system, strictly speaking, God is not the highest reality. It is only an appearance. The highest reality is *nirguṇa Brahman* and since God is relational, it is related to a lower position. In the light of this, it is wrong to overemphasise on the need of God's grace in attaining *mokṣa*. So goes the criticism. *Paramācārya* is not prepared to accept this criticism. He would simply dismiss it as purely theoretical and dry. For all practical purposes, *Brahman* is God and it manifests itself as world. We have to reach the ideal of Advaita through Dvaita. As *paramācārya* beautifully puts it, even the Advaita outlook one gains through the grace of God.

The next question to be considered is how to preserve *dharma*? The answer of *paramācārya* is quick and direct. By following its tenets and practices. In his clear words:

> If our religion is in danger, it is not because of other religions. On the contrary, it is due to the lack of religious practices on our side.[3]

He continues:

> If we scrupulously adhere to the religious practices, someone among us will become perfect and the presence of one perfect human is strength and solace to others who live with him or her and religion will be taken care of.[4] The way to strength which is long and hard lies through moral and scriptural practices (*anuṣṭhāna*).[5]

Paramācārya, here, puts more emphasis on preserving the essence of Vedic religion as it enables an individual to lead a disciplined life. Vedic religion is interested in making man perfect and for this it calls upon every individual to perform one's duties (*karmānuṣṭhāna*); to cultivate cardinal virtues (*śīla*); to worship the deity (*upāsanā*); and to acquire wisdom (*jñāna*). For all this, the mind should be purified.

Now, the social perspective of the *paramācārya* may be outlined. Advaita as religion is interested in exploring the highest value in every individual. The highest value is called *mokṣa* or liberation. It acts, according to *paramācārya*, as a basis of social action. Due to ignorance man identifies himself with body and that is the

> starting point of all misery. *Mokṣa* consists in renouncing this false identification. The individual then comes out of the meshes of *Saṁsāra* and realises his true nature as *Satcidānanda*.

Thus liberation of the Self is the *summum bonum* of life, according to *paramācārya*. This, however, does not mean that in Advaita Vedānta there is no concern for social ethics and development. Advaita certainly attaches great significance to social ethics and moral development. This is very much stressed by the *paramācārya* when he says that our life, right from the Vedas, has really cared for social relevance. It has always concentrated on *dharma*, which is the very basis of society. *Dharma* ordains individuals to lead a good life, which in turn gives *abhyudaya*, or social welfare. *Abhyudaya* consists in the effective control and development of the individual. *Niśreyasa* or Self-realisation goes side by side with *dharma* as it is an ingredient of *dharma*. One who realises both *abhyudaya* and *niśreyasa* becomes the spiritual leader of society. Under his far-sightedness and able guidance, the social life of the individual gets elated and elevated. There takes place transvaluation of all social values with orientation to *mokṣa*, the *summum bonum*, avers *paramācārya*.

The Advaitic concepts like *sādhana catuṣṭaya*, *brahmātmaikya jñāna* have important social significance. Properly analysed they point to the social well-being of man. *Paramācārya* was fond of quoting *Īśa Upaniṣad*: "Enjoy life with a spirit of detachment". One should remain in the world judiciously enjoying it; at the same time one should remain untouched by it. He should invariably work, but with a sense of detachment. The real happiness consists in denying the ego. The social thought of the Hindu tradition believes in owning the whole world but not in owing the ego. The teaching of the *paramācārya* is no exception to this! One should renounce not life, but selfishness in the interest of *niśreyasa*, the highest ideal. *Brahman*, which is termed *nirañjana*, is none other than the individual self. Hence both *abhyudaya* and *niśreyasa*, are accommodated duly in Advaita Vedānta. *Tyāga* or renunciation of the petty self is the fulcrum of the social philosophy of *paramācārya*.

What has *paramācārya* to say about *varṇa-dharma*, and *varṇāśrama-dharma*, the major social concepts of Hindu life? *Paramācārya* lost no time in pointing out that *varṇāśrama-dharma* is the very basis of Hindu society. The literal meaning of the word *varṇa* is 'to choose' or 'select'. Depending upon the dominance of the *triguṇa*s, namely *sattva*, *rajas* and *tamas*, one's *varṇa* is going to be determined. *Paramācārya* is bent upon saying that *varṇa-dharma* should never be equated with *jāti*, which has divided and sub-divided the society into small non-harmonious disintegrating segments. In addition to *varṇa-dharma* or *viśeṣa dharma*, Hindu philosophy also vehemently postulates and advocates what are called *sādhāraṇa dharma*s or common duties to be followed by all members of society, irrespective of their *varṇa*, like *satya* (truth), *ahiṁsā* (non-violence) and *karuṇā* (kindness). The common duties presuppose the Advaita base, the unity of all human beings.

Āśrama-dharma is a carefully-designed framework primarily put forward and advocated by Hinduism, keeping individuals' liberation in mind. The literal meaning of the word *āśrama* is 'to put effort' or to halt at regular intervals in preparation to reach a higher stage in life. Roughly they may be called 'stages in life' by following which the individual is led regularly (*kramaśaḥ*) to the highest end, namely *mokṣa*. The four stages of life are: *brahmacarya* (studentship), *gr̥hastha* (householder), *vānaprastha* (forest dweller) and *saṁnyāsa* (wandering monk). Each stage is equally important, providing the necessary requirement to climb the next higher stage in the ladder of life and finally getting oneself released from the cycle of birth and death (*mokṣa*). While laying emphasis on *saṁnyāsa*, Advaita points out that the importance of the other three *āśrama*s should not be lost sight of.

What is true *mokṣa*? According to *paramācārya*, it is not a post-mortem state. It is the eternal nature of the Self. *Jīvanmukti* is the true *mukti*. It is the realisation of *Brahman*-knowledge, experienced in one's own heart, while bearing a body.[6] *Paramācārya* is happy to note that Śaṅkara's message is all-comprehensive and soul-making. It is at once remarkable. He extols the importance of Śaṅkara to the trouble-torn world and the relevance of his message. He says:

> If one wishes to know the Real one should study the *ācārya*'s works. Is it possible to measure his greatness?[7]

When do acts become sinful? When *sādhāraṇa dharma*s are ignored. Also when actions are performed for selfish interests, avers *paramācārya*. He advises the devotees to let love be the sole motive. Passions such as desire and hatred, anger and malice must be totally conquered. If love becomes the guiding principle of all deeds then most of the ills of the world will vanish. *Paramācārya* was such a great saint that mere uttering of his sacred name is suffice to purify and sanctify man's life. He was himself a living scripture.

What is the necessity of moral and spiritual discipline? *Paramācārya* asserts that it is for attaining *mokṣa*. He asks his followers to treat this life as the last one. One should perform *niṣkāma karma* and put maximum effort, so that one overcomes next birth. In other words, in this life itself, one should strive to get liberated from the fetters of *saṁsāra*. For that self-control, self-help and self-culture should take a front seat. They are very essential for self-development. Vedānta, the end of the Vedas, teaches the way for the removal of sorrow. If there is another, there is desire, hatred and fear. If there is no second then there is no hatred or fear. Absolute Reality, thus, is the basis of the whole world.

Regarding sainthood there are misconceptions. One such misconception is that the saints are uncommon and supernormal. They are indifferent to pricking realities of life. In one word, they are super-individualistic.[8] This is not true to the core as far as *paramācārya* is concerned. He was an embodiment of kindness and compassion. He was a self-controlled *puruṣa*. He was the same in pain and pleasure. He was friendly and at the same time fearless.

There is another question. It is related to performance of miracles. Should miracles and sainthood go together? This is a difficult question to answer. The popular view is that a saint should perform at least some miracles. They should exhibit some supernatural and supernormal powers. It is believed that in the life of some saints such miracles as walking on water, sitting on fire, cooling flames, walking upward in the sky and performing alchemy, have occurred. But this is only as the devotees see sainthood. To expect every saint to perform a miracle is a misconception. In fact, a true saint does not attach importance to such supernatural powers. Often he considers them as hindrances in the way of spiritual progress. The devotees should guard themselves against such circus arts; the saints themselves warn. The saints, on the other hand, are virtuous. They are liberal-minded persons. Compassion is the princely virtue with them. They are the fit instruments of social service.[9] They belong to all mankind. They have inspired social reform. They are the embodiments of god's vision and all the good in life. In them there is the confluence of head and heart. They lead a dedicated and unselfish life. They have wisdom, devotion and self-control. Love is the centre of their life.

The question remains. What miracle did *paramācārya* perform? Not the populist but an inner one, in my view, and that consists in his mastery over the fund of knowledge found in the body of Vedānta. And in his life the ideal of *guru*, as enunciated by Śrī Śaṅkara, is fulfilling. "Who is a *guru*? He who has realised the truth and who is always intent on the disciple's good". *Paramācārya* lived up to this ideal without levying even an iota of doubt. He fulfilled the noble spiritual mission entrusted to him by Śrī Śaṅkara. Through inner awakening he championed the cause of human development. His life was a ceaseless and untiring effort at stabilising and promoting the spirit of India. It can be said that he has moved the world one step further towards spiritual development. Is there any other miracle higher than this!

Paramācārya, to conclude, served as a beacon of light for the spiritual guidance of all devotees. He was a *jīvanmukta*. He was bent on uplifting *dharma*. He was looked upon with utmost veneration for the penance he did for *loka-kalyāṇa*. The Śrī Kāñcī Kāmakoṭi Pīṭha and the *guru* shed lustre on each other. He lived the most complete simplistic life. He had a saving grace. He had intense concern for the lowliest and the last. His life was a saga of untiring dedication to the holy task of fulfilling the lofty spiritual mission of humanism. Like Lord Dakṣiṇāmūrty he realised truth as a *maunī* (observer of Truth in silence) but when he spoke, it was from the level of inward experience. He was the replica, so to say, of ancient wisdom. In short, he was a person of perfect self-detachment, a *mahāpuruṣa* of unbounded love.

Reference

1. T.M.P. Mahadevan, *The Saints of India*, 965, Preface.
2. *Preceptors of Advaita,* 1968, p. 535.
3. Quoted by Prof. R. Balasubramanian in *The Voice of Śaṅkara*, special vol. 18, no. 1, Jan, 1993, Chennai. p. 172.
4. *The Voice of Śaṅkara* — special. vol. 18, no. 1.
5. *Ibid.*

6. *Brahma-sūtra*, IV, 1-15.
7. *Preceptors of Advaita*, Quoted by T.M.P. Mahadevan introduction.
8. T.M.P. Mahadevan, *The Saints of India*, p. 17.
9. *The Saints of India*.

14

Sri Nijaguna Sivayogi: Mysticism

B.P. Siddhashrama

THE mysticism of Sri Nijaguna Sivayogi, who was a philosopher, a poet, a composer of music, a musicologist and a mystic of great spiritual originality, is described in the following paragraphs. Nijaguna Sivayogi, who is a great philosopher-mystic from Karnataka, has written eight philosophical works in Kannaḍa.

Mysticism is the philosophy of self-realisation and/or God-realisation, which implies and involves the faculty of intuition, which in turn is the supra-sensory and supra-mental experience that is aroused in us by proper spiritual intuition and practice. Mysticism is a power which directly and immediately perceives, touches, and hears the all-pervading Reality. Further, mysticism is a noetic and ineffable experience in which the subject-object distinction is transcended and submerged.

There are mainly four forms of mysticism accepted by modern philosophers of mysticism. They are: (1) Theistic Mysticism, (2) Absolutistic Mysticism, (3) Introversive Mysticism, and (4) Extroversive Mysticism. Not all the four forms are found in a mystic normally. But Nijaguna's conception of mystical experience incorporates all the four forms of mysticism. This shows the catholicity of Sri Nijaguna Sivayogi for although Nijaguna is an Advaitin, is essentially in favour of Absolute or Identity Mysticism, he nevertheless does not totally reject the other forms of mysticism. For instance he allows Theistic Mysticism for *mandādhikarīs* (minimally fit) and *madhyamādhikārīs* (moderately fit). For the optimally fit and the maximally fit he prescribes only Absolute Mysticism. Nijaguna has not differentiated between the means and forms of mysticism. Actually the different means of *yoga*s prescribed by Nijaguna for the attainment of mystical experience are different forms of mystical experience as well. Nijaguna has discussed 21 *yoga*s in his works. Here only six prominent *yoga*s of Nijaguna are explained.

The six means or yogas

Nijaguna has prescribed six *yoga*s in the *Yoga-prati-pādana-sthala* of *Kaivalya Paddhati*, the *paramārtha gīte* and the *paramānubhava bodhe*, which aim at restraining the mind-stuff from taking various forms and lead the mind towards msystical trance. The six *yoga*s are: (1) *mantra-yoga*, (2) *laya-yoga*, (3) *haṭha-yoga*, (4) *rāja-yoga*, (5) *śīva-yoga* (6) *nirguṇāṣṭāṅga-yoga*.

MANTRA-YOGA

There are two forms of *mantra-yoga*: (1) *japa-mantra-yoga*, and (2) *ajapā-mantra-yoga*. The *japa-mantra-yoga* consists in doing repeated *japa* of *mantra*s like *oṁ namasśivāya* and *hrīṁ hrāṁ hrūṁ namasśivāya,* which are addressed to different chosen deities and getting meditatively absorbed in those respective deities. The *ajapā-mantra-yoga* consists in methodically, meditatively following through the *so'ham mantra* the natural course of our breathing, which according to Nijaguna, takes place 21,600 times a day. Nijaguna says that while taking the breath inside, the word *soḥ* and while leaving the breath, the word *haṁ:* emerge naturally; if we put it as *haṁsoḥ* it signifies *jīva* and if we reverse its order it reads as and signifies *so'haṁ*, meaning 'That-Thou-Art'. If we remove *soḥ* and *haḥ* what remains is *oṁ* (the *praṇava mantra*) which emerges in *bhrū-madhya* (the mid-brow). This is the modification of the *so'ham mantra*, the metaphysical import of which is: if we leave the *māyopādhi īśvara* (*sa*) and *avidyopādhi jīva* (*ha*) what remains is pure-consciousness (i.e., *oṁ*). Nijaguna says that by concentrating, reflecting and meditating on this *ajapā-mantra* one can attain *samādhi.*[1]

LAYA-YOGA

The *laya-yoga* consists in the total dissolution of mind along with the *prāṇa-vāyu* (the life breath), either in the *anāhata-nāda*, i.e., the uninterrupted and continuous inner sound within one's ears or in the *bindu* (the focal point) of Inner Light within one's eyes. [Graphically describing the *modus operandi* of the *laya-yoga*, Nijaguna says as follows. Having a quiescent mind one should perform *japa* of *mantra* and should see different kinds of Light like the Garland of Lightening, the Sparkles of Gold, the Constellation of Shining Stars, the Glowing Halo of the Sun, the Moon and the Fire, etc., in one's own Mid-brow. Then one should listen to the different *anāhata-nādas* (Uninterrupted sounds), like the Constant-Drumming-Sound of the Ocean, the Thundering Sound of the Clashing Clouds and the Divine Sound of Conchs and Bells.] And then one should dissolve one's self totally in the *nitya-nirmala-sat-cit-ānanda-śambhuliṅga* who alone remains after the *vilaya* or dissolution of all lights, darkness, sounds, the sun-moon and the stars and the entire universe of name and form.[2]

HAṬHA-YOGA

The *haṭha-yoga*, according to Nijaguna, consists in the conquest of breath and mind through the *aṣṭāṅga-yoga* of *yama*, *niyama*, *āsana*, *prāṇāyāma*, *pratyāhāra*, *dhāraṇā* and *samādhi* and through the six *kāraṇas* of *bastī*, *dhauti*, *neti*, *trāṭaka*, *nauli* and *kapālabhāti* and through the *mudrās* of *khecarī*, *bhūcari*, *śāmbhavī*, *ṣaṇmukhī*, etc., and through the *kumbhaka*.[3]

RĀJA-YOGA

The *rāja-yoga* consists in the firm and stable concentration of one's mind by realising the true nature of the Self through the three *lakṣyas* (or the focal-objectives) of (1) the inner-*lakṣyas*, (2) the middle-*lakṣyas* and (3) the outer-*lakṣyas* of the mind.[4]

ŚIVA-YOGA

The *śiva-yoga* consists in the five steps of (1) the worship of who is of the nature of *guru*, (2) the meditation of the identity of one's Self with Śiva, (3) the Unparalleled Loving-Devotion to Śiva, (4) realisation of the true nature of Śiva, and (5) the observance of sacred *Śiva-vrata*s (Śiva-Rites).[5]

NIRGUṆĀṢṬĀṄGA-YOGA

Nijaguṇa has adapted the Patañjali's *Aṣṭāṅga-yoga* to the Advaitic-Mystical practice (which is his unique contribution both to the *yoga* and to Advaitic Mysticism) which he has called *nirguṇāṣṭāṅga-yoga*. *Nirguṇāṣṭāṅga-yoga* consists of the following steps:

(i) *Yama*, says Nijaguna, consists in getting *vairāgya* about one's own body, senses and mind, etc., as they are all *anātma*s.

(ii) *Niyama* consists in making the above *vairāgya* stand firmly in one's mind.

(iii) *Āsana* is that state of mind which is *udāsīna* of (indifferent to) both *rāga* (attachment) and *virāga* (detachment).

(iv) *Prāṇāyāma* is the total stoppage of the *adhyāsika* relationship with the body, the senses, etc.

(v) *Pratyāhāra* consists in the total withdrawal of the mind from the objective world and in the directing of it towards *ātman* within.

(vi) *Dhāraṇā* consists in the fixing of the mind, that has thus turned within, firmly on pure-*cit*.

(vii) *Dhyāna* consists in the meditation of the mind that is thus firmly fixed on pure-*cit*, on its nature as pure-*cit*.

(viii) *Samādhi* is the state where the above meditative Self (the *dhyānākāravr̥tti*) totally submerges itself in pure-*cit* and becomes its pure essential form (*svarūpākāravr̥tti*). This state is called *turīya*. This *turīya* state emerges out of the *nirguṇāṣṭāṅga-yoga*. It is of the form of *svarūpākāra-vr̥tti* or *ātmākāra-vr̥tti* and hence is not the ultimate state. The ultimate or final state is the next state which is *turīyātīta* in which all the *vṛttis*, including the *svarūpākāra-vṛtti*, are dissolved and the intrinsic universal pure-*cit* shines in itself.[6] This state is also called by Nijaguna as the state of *niravaraṇa samādhi*. According to Nijaguna the *turīya* state of *samādhi* can be attained through the *sarvātmaka* (extrovertive) method. The *yogī* who attains this *samādhi* is called by Nijaguna as *vaiyākaraṇī*, who out of his pure love for his fellow being engages himself in teaching and uplifting his fellow beings. The last *turīyātīta* state of *samādhi* can, according to Nijaguna, be attained through the *netyātmaka* (introvertive) method. In this state the *yogī* is called *maunī* for he is always silently in his *samādhi* and never descends to *vyutthāna*.[7]

The six forms of samādhi

Nijaguna, the great mystic, describes six different forms of *samādhi*,[8] apparently from his own mystical experience. Of these six forms four belong to the *savikalpa-samādhi* (which, according to Nijaguna, refers to the *turīya* state) and two to the *nirvikalpa samādhi* (which, according to Nijaguna, refers to the *turīyātīta* state). The six forms of *samādhi* are as follows:

ANTAR-DṚŚYĀNUVEDA-SAVIKALPA-SAMĀDHI

Mental *vṛttis* like *kāmākāra-vṛttis* and *krodhākāra-vṛttis*, are the internal (*antar*) *vṛttis* which are witnessed by *sākṣī*. And if one contemplates that he is only the *sākṣī* who transcends all those internal *vṛttis* and who is identical with *Brahman* and gets *samādhi*, one is said to have attained *antar-dṛśyānuveda-savikalpa-samādhi*.

ANTAR-ŚABDĀNUVEDA-SAVIKALPA-SAMĀDHI

After from the *guru* the *tat tvam asi* and other *mahāvākyas*, if one annihilates the *upādhis* of both *Īśvara* and *jīva* and realises the identity of *Brahman* and *ātman*, contemplates on it and gets *samādhi*, one is said to have attained *antar-śabdānuveda-śavikalpa-śamādhi.*

ANTAR-NIRVIKALPA-SAMĀDHI

The Bliss that emerges from the above two *samādhis* is the Bliss of the *pratibimba*. The Bliss of the *bimba*, however, cannot be experienced because it is of the nature of the Experience. Hence it can only be inferred from the Bliss of the *pratibimba*. Therefore what, after transcending the above two *samādhis*, "remains like a lamp which is kept where there is absolutely no movement of air" is called *antar-nirvikalpa-samādhi.*

BĀHYA-DṚŚYĀNUVEDA-SAVIKALPA-SAMĀDHI

When one dissociates the name and form from external objects into which one's *vṛttis* enter and contemplates only on *asti*, *bhāti* and *priya* of those objects (which are *Brahma-aṁśas*) and attains *samādhi*, one is said to have attained *bāhya-dṛśyānuveda-savikalpa-samādhi*. In this *samādhi* one sees only the *Brahman* and not the world of external objects.

BĀHYA-ŚABDĀNUVEDA-SAVIKALPA-SAMĀDHI

After listening to the *guru* about the *Brahman* as being of the nature of *sat*, *cit* and *ānanda* if one contemplates on that nature of *Brahman*, one's *vṛttis* become the *brahmākāra-vṛttis* and this state is called *bāhya-śabdānuveda-savikalpa-samādhi*.

BĀHYA-NIRVIKALPA-SAMĀDHI

By rising above the *bāhya-dṛśyānuveda-savikalpa-samādhi* and *bāhya-śabdānuveda-savikalpa-samādhi* if one transcends the subject-object-distinction and submerges one's Self into the Integral-one-ness and remains peacefully like the waveless ocean, one is said to have attained the *bāhya-nirvikalpa-samādhi.*

Through the practice of the above six *yogas* and *samādhis* the *sādhaka* will get himself submerged in the Absolute Reality and see everywhere only the *śambhuliṅga* or *Brahman*. This, according to Sri Nijaguna Sivayogi, is the Advaitic mystic path, which leads one to Infinity or *mokṣa*.

Reference

1. *Yogapratipādana Sthala of Kaivalya Paddhati*, 5.
2. *Ibid.*, 6.
3. *Ibid.*, 4, 3.
4. *Yogapratipādana Sthala of Kaivalya Paddhati*, 4, 4 and for more details see, 18.
5. For details see, *ibid.*, 4-5.
6. *Paramāṇubhava bodhe*, 4.19.8.
7. *Ibid.*, 6.11.10.
8. *Anubhava Sāra*, 6.4 and *Viveka Cintāmaṇi*, pp. 52-3.

15

Prajapita Brahma: Rāja-yoga

S.C. Suguna Kumari

THE movement of Prajapita Brahma, the founding father of Prajapita Brahma Kumari University, is a unique religious and social phenomenon. The Prajapita Brahma Kumari University is not an academic university but an institution for spiritual training, moral rejuvenation and transformation of the individual. The founder of this movement was an ordinary businessman, but a spiritually motivated person. Towards the end of his mortal career, he was destined to experience a series of mystic visions — the form of God as a point of Light, man's perfect highest form, and the end of this is a world. And out of this chaos also emerged a New World order in which beauty, purity, and truth prevail. This vision transformed the life of the founder of this movement and resulted in the formation of a new Hindu religious order.

The aim of this spiritual programme is to enable the human being to fully develop spiritual well-being through *rāja-yoga*. Another objective of this *yoga* is peace and tranquillity for humanity. Spiritual education imparted in this informal university concentrates on realising the Supreme Soul, the nature of the three worlds, the history of time, such as coming into being and going out of it of all things in creation. A complete understanding of the ethical and spiritual meaning of human life is the cardinal virtue of Prajapita Brahma's teaching.

Admission into this order is available for all those who are spiritually inclined. Anyone can participate in this order and there is no discrimination due to caste, creed, religion, class, race or country. The principal objective of this movement is to obtain peace of mind. Towards this end, the practice of *rāja-yoga* is made easy for the common man. Interestingly women occupy a pre-eminent position in this organisation. Women who dedicate their services for the promotion of the ideals of Prajapita Brahma are titled as Brahma-Kumaris or the 'Daughters of Brahma'. They are in full-time service in this spiritual mission, leaving behind their worldly connections including their family. It is a new social reformation movement with compassion for women's education, the great vision of Prajapita Brahma. The founder has rightly realised that women are well-suited for religious orders, as they are embodiments of patience, dedication and persuasion.

Prajapita Brahma was concerned with the plight of humanity like any true religious leader. The cause for this conflict and despair in human society is due to ignorance about the nature of Self. Humanity is reeling in conflict, violence and hatred due to negative thinking. This Spiritual Order stresses on the role and power of human mind. They are more powerful than actions. They are the seeds of action. Thoughts unfailingly bring their appropriate result. In this connection Prajapita Brahma opines that the world today is witnessing tremendous conflicts due to divisions of many kinds. The power of purity and righteousness will help restore peace and equanimity. Pure feelings — feeling of love and brotherhood — alone can bring necessary changes for peace and survival in this world.

Prajapita Brahma has outlined a programme of spiritual practice for bringing love and happiness in the world through the meditation of *rāja-yoga*. It is also known as remembering God. This method of *yoga* is a renewal and continuation of the ancient classical form of *rāja-yoga*, which was emphasised in the teachings of Vivekananda and others. One has to allow his mind with the help of *rāja-yoga* to know the Supreme Father, the Supreme Soul in one's life. The Supreme Father is the divine architect of this creation. The Supreme Soul is the dwelling spirit in the human being in Prajapita Brahma's philosophy. These two are separate from each other and one cannot be reduced to the other. It is a kind of Dvaita philosophy, a life of spiritual dualism.

The Supreme Father is not a human being in any anthropomorphic sense; symbolically he is a father who protects and governs. He is the source of all energy. This energy is known through meditation upon a form of Light as its focus. It is a point, a perfect form of the highest concentration. It is easy to experience this godly perfection. He also defined this as a *yajña*, in which one has to sacrifice all vices.

Prajapita Brahma expounded on some of the discourses of *Bhagavad Gītā*, as a prelude to his *rāja-yoga* technique. Before we go to the interpretation of the *Gītā* as pronounced by Prajapita Brahma let us look at the *rāja-yoga* meditation, the cornerstone of the founder's revelation. *Rāja-yoga* is the surest means of obtaining control over one's affairs of life. Undesirable and impure thoughts which aggravate the behaviour of man are systematically brought under control. With stress and anxiety removed from life, peace prevails. It is an effortless form of meditation which shows the nature of Self in its perfect form.

Prajapita Brahma's revaluation of this *rāja-yoga* should not be construed as one more modern technique to reveal to modern man, who is impatient of everything around him, the existence of Holy God and meaning of life. This *yoga* is based on the ancient understanding of the powers of the mind, which was realised by all those great sages of India. *Rāja-yoga* enhances Self-knowledge, which creates the power of concentration to perceive the source of Light, the greatest mystic experience. This *rāja-yoga* is for everybody, whoever is interested in peace and interpersonal relationship. Prajapita Brahma introduced to all and sundry, the pleasures of mystic life without alienating them from normal human relationships and social obligations. It is a training to transform oneself into spiritual excellence.

Prajapita Brahma relied upon the spiritual messages of *Bhagavad Gītā* to design the *rāja-yoga* techniques. Human life is the last in the cycle of rebirths. The message of *Gītā* is to realise the importance of this life and act appropriately. Prajapita Brahma voiced that the Lord Kṛṣṇa, the divine sermoniser of the *Gītā*, is coming again to redeem this world of sin and suffering. In reality the Supreme Father bestowed the knowledge of *Gītā* long before Lord Kṛṣṇa expounded it to Arjuna. The message of *Gītā* is not limited to one age, place and person. It is an eternal message. War, violence and fight are not the essences of *Gītā* as is commonly misunderstood. The war is within the human being and peace is the victory. Human being is expected to constantly meditate upon the nature of true Self to conquer passion.

Celibacy and vegetarianism are highly recommended as they are conducive for the practice of this *yoga*. Prajapita Brahma expounded in his discourses not only the true message of the *Bhagavad Gītā*, but also the relationship between Self and God and Śīva and Śaṅkara, inner dynamics of *karma*, conquest of death and God Realisation.

This religious organisation has received appreciation from the United Nations General Assembly as a valid means in the pursuit of peace. It is one of the best examples of national integration as it involves spiritual traffic from Mount Abu in all directions of the country and extending internationally in pursuit of inter-religious understanding. The message of Prajapita Brahma is not an isolated voice; instead it is strongly rooted in the traditions of the Vedas, Upaniṣads and Purāṇas.

Let us recapitulate our understanding of Prajapita Brahma's mission and message so far enumerated. It aims at easing tension and anxiety, improving power of concentration, memory and intelligence, bringing changes in human behaviour. It is also sought to apply in schools for the benefit of students, to workers in all walks of life and to all members of society not leaving anti-social and morally debased persons. Education is the main thrust of this movement. Education has to be understood in a broad sense as involving the spiritual side and character building and not just being time-bound book-learning. It is meant to create awareness among people so that they can solve their personal, social and psychological conflicts. A higher degree of mental composure, work efficiency and ease in social dynamics for successful human interaction, are the priorities of this mission. One should not be hasty and label the spirit of this mission as exclusively religious. This order, which started in a humble way inspired by the revelations of its founder, has grown with more than three thousand branches all over the world. It is a rare religious organisation which gives priority and importance to women in organisational capacities. The present head of the international religious organisation is a woman, the spiritually distinguished Udaya Mohin. As Victor Turner very ably expounded, we find in this cult aspects of "status elevation and status reversal". The emphasis of this mission is on moral character and personality development. Prajapita Brahma did not separate religion from social, political and economic dimensions of life. It is one of the living and practising Hindu religious creeds upholding the age-old values of *rāja-yoga*.

16

Sri Satya Sai Cult of Love and Devotion

G. Sundara Ramaiah
&
S.D.A. Joga Rao

In this paper a very humble attempt is made to understand and critically appreciate the religion, philosophy and culture that is being developed in 'Prasantinilayam', the earthly abode of Bhagavan Sri Satya Sai Baba. Born on 23 November 1926, at Puttaparti, a very tiny village in Anantapur District of Andhra Pradesh nearer to Bangalore, Baba was regarded as a 'Miracle Man', an 'Organiser of Hindu Religion', an 'Incarnation of Love and Wisdom' and 'A Saviour of the Suffering'. Comparing himself with the eternally radiating sun, which gives light to one and all whether they ask for it or not, Baba said:

> The Lord is like the sun. When his rays fall upon your heart, moving the clouds of egoism, the lotus bud blooms and the petals unfold. Remember, only the buds that are ready will bloom, the rest will have to wait patiently.

This reminds us what the great Vedāntin, Śrī Madhvācārya had said about the "selection and rejection of the souls by God". Many people, when finding themselves in the presence of Satya Sai Baba, have experienced a tremendous opening of the heart, a warmth stirring into understanding, a melting of the dryness that was constricting them — they start to wonder, who is this being who can do this to me.

If it is asked 'who is Satya Sai Baba', we get not one answer but several answers — not conflicting with each other but transporting us from one bewilderment to another. The outward descriptions are deceptive. Yet one can describe his outward form, the saffron-coloured gown, the feet without sandals, and the very simple life he leads. But that is not Sai. He is a form or a figure in which love abides. He is the embodiment of Love or, as someone prefers to call, he is 'Love walking on two legs', teaching devotion to one and all to cultivate equanimity of mind (*samatva sāmyān bhakti yoga*). Love is God and God is love, says Sai. Gandhi's famous saying, "God is Truth and Truth is God" approximates this. Just as Jesus Christ had demonstrated the truth contained in the above saying, Sai Baba has rightly demonstrated it both in precept and concept.

Sai Baba: Is he a man of miracles?

The answer is an emphatic yes. What is a miracle? A miracle is a violation of Law. Can a man violate it? No. Can nature violate herself? We do not know. It is their ambivalent situation that gives us a chance to believe in the possibility of miracles. A miracle is not a trick, it is not an illusion. It is divine will interacting with the cosmic forces, which is beyond the understanding of ordinary persons. His countless miracles such as raising the dead, curing the incurable (by modern medicine), and producing golden ornaments, *vibhūti*, flowers and *akṣantalu* and so on has demonstrated his powers over nature. But this is not his mission. This is not his cult. This is not the culture of the Sai. If he has constantly manifested things out of thin air, revealed the past and the future of everyone, and constantly responded to the calls of his devotees, it only goes to show that he shares the divine quality of omniscience.

You may perhaps do not believe all this that we are saying. Neither have we any intention of asking you to believe all this. Just as Lord Buddha said *Ātmā Dīpobhava* (Let Thyself Shine), Sai Baba says: "Come investigate, ascertain for yourself. My activities are open to the scrutiny of all".

One has to judge Sai Baba not from his miracles but from his 'actions'. Sai Baba is a real *karma-yogī*, befitting all the descriptions of a *karma-yogī* given in the *Bhagavad Gītā*. A closer association with the Sai Baba has enabled us to arrive at the conviction that he is:

(i) an *ātmāvalokin,* (ii) a *jñāna-yogin,* (iii) a *yoga-yukta,* (iv) a *viśuddhātmā,* (v) a *vijñānātmā,* (vi) a *vimuktātmā,* (vii) a *jitendriya*, *jita-krodha*, and a (viii) *sarvabhūtāntarātmabhāvaka*

Therefore he is, for the devotees, *bhagavān*.

Whatever programme such a *karma-yogī* undertakes will necessarily have a divine touch, for they are all done for the sake of universal welfare and well-being. Witness, for example, the various organisations which he has created and which he has ensured would work with sincerity, ability and dignity coupled with morality.

The most inspiring organisation is the *sevādal*. Here people forget their rank and file and are prepared to do any service to the other man with cheerfulness and brimming with love and affection and overflowing with an in-built discipline. Here in this organisation discipline comes from within — not from authority, fear of law or compunction, but out of love towards the fellow beings. Sai says Love is God. Anything, which we do with love, is to participate in the quality of God. Sai Baba's teachings on love remind us of the famous discussion of Yajñavalkya with Gārgı in the *Bṛhadārṇyaka Upaniṣad*, which reads thus:

> Under the mighty rule of this immutable, O Gargi, the sun and the moon are held in their positions. Under the mighty rule of their immutable O Gargi, heaven and earth maintain their positions; under the mighty rule of this immutable *muharta*s, days and nights, fortnights, months, seasons and years are held in their respective places . . . O Gargi! men praise those that give, the gods depend on the sacrificer, and the manes on independent offerings.
>
> — III.viii.9. Mādhavānanda's Translation, pp. 519-20

It is this mighty love that animates, sustains and upholds nature. The ferocious tiger, the meek lamb and the wicked man all participate in it and abide in it in their moments of realisation of inner bliss. Though humanity is suffering with want and need, Baba says there is within it a fountain of joy and bliss and if they have to manifest in human actions, love is the instrument. The key to the treasure of human amity (*a-vaira bhāva* and *mitra bhāva*), says Sai Baba, is love. Love is Sai. To love Sai is to love your fellow being. Hear to serve the fellow men, before you begin to serve the Divine Sai, says Sai. He reminds us of our moral and social responsibilities. While saving the world from the natural calamities is the duty of God, saving the society from human calamities is the foremost duty of man. The famous Biblical saying, "Love thy neighbour" is transformed and transfigured in the activities of the Sevādal and Bālavikās, the two mighty organisations of Sai Baba. He says:

> Your duty is to keep calm (*Mauna*), to pray for the welfare and happiness of all. You are an organic part of one human global family (*Vasudhaiva Kutumbam*). Share your Love with others (since you will not prefer to share your wealth with others). Sharing of Love with others will endure you forever. Keep the company of the good and avoid the evil company and then Love flows automatically.

Spreading of Universal Love (viśva mānava prema)

Sai wants all his devotees to promote love and discard hatred. The fragrance of love can travel any distance, whereas the chemical perfumes, however loveable they may be, suffer from limitations of space and time. To be strong one has to be fair, to be fair one has to be moral, and to be moral one should abide in love. Speaking on the evils of the contemporary civilisation, Sai Baba cautions us not to fail to notice the veils of immorality. He says:

> Immorality has put on the cloak of morality and is taking man into the pit of sin. Truth is condemned as a trap,

justice is scoffed at, saints and godly persons are slandered as social nuisances.

The task of the present *avatāra*, says Baba, is to love the good and reform the wicked. The function of the previous *avatāra*s was to put away with the evil persons. But Sai *avatāra*, an *avatāra* of Love, is to take the wicked into the fold of the divine arms and extend love, so that they will get transformed into lovable creatures. History of religions proves this, says Baba. Aṅgulimāla, Aśoka, Bimbisāra, Vālmikī had received the bliss of the Divine Love and got themselves merged in it. Sai Baba says that God has to take on human form and rescue man from his own destructive nature. And by destroying man, the wickedness that resides in him cannot be wiped out because he will reborn again as a wicked man by the propensity of wickedness. Therefore Sai Baba says Love is a powerful divine mechanism which can do extraordinary things. And these are countless by him, to attract people to the glory of the God. Millions visit Him each year, and millions return home to do their best to live up to the *ādeśa*, *upadeśa* and *saṅdeśa* of Sai.

Now we shall discuss six important action-oriented programmes that Sai Baba has commissioned: (a) internalisation of the devotees who visit him; (b) socialisation of all the members of the Sai Cult; (c) moralisation of all the educational programmes; (d) acculturisation of the devotees; (e) spiritualisation of the devotees; and (f) divinisation programme.

(a) The internalisation programmes are intended for and aimed at the reformation of the individual both at the psychological and physical (bodily) levels.

(b) The socialisation programmes help in harmonious development of society and include programmes that help to keep the society in concordance and remove the discordant elements in society, not by force but by change in the attitude, will and voluntary submission to work and to God.

(c) Moralisation programmes are intended not to be coloured

with morality but to really transform the inner psyche of the individual devotee.

(d) Acculturisation of the individual involves those kinds of programmes that keep the individual and society going as a cultural centre in which every individual takes part and builds up his own culture and social culture. Herein the individual is tangent to cultivate and practice virtues like *ahiṁsā*, *dharma*, *satya*, *śauca*, *maitrī*, *karuṇā*, *namratā*, *śīla*, *śikṣā*, *vinaya*, *saundarya*, *saddharma*, *nirbhayatva* and so on.

(e) Spiritualisation programme is intended to generate *dhi-śakti* and *ātma-śakti* (intellectual powers and soul-power); *prajñā-śakti*, *abhaya-śakti* and *tyāga-śīlatā* are cultivated here.

(f) Divinisation programme is intended to realise Viṣṇu, Nārāyaṇa, Vasudeva, Buddha, Allāh, Jesus — all names of the Supreme God.

Spirituality is not about cosiness, comfort and security. We need to come out of ourselves, expand our horizon, grow and take the opportunities given. Let us take an interest in the wider picture. This is surely what Swami is asking and doing. He says human values and values of commodities are inversely proportional.

Swamiji's views on women are quite interesting. Asked by a sincere devotee, "Who is greater in the creation — Man or Woman?", Sai Baba said:

> It is said in the *Bhagavad Gītā* that man is endowed with three powers, while woman is bestowed with seven. Thus woman is on a higher plane.

The word *strī* (woman) comprises three letters — *sa*, *ta*, *ra*. *Sa* stands for *sāttvika* qualities, *ta* denotes *tāmasika* qualities and *ra* stands for *rājasika* qualities, says Baba. All the three qualities put together enable the women to possess many more qualities than man. Endurance, calmness and patience (*orpu* and *kṣamā*) represent the *sāttvika* qualities, which are but natural to a woman.

The *rājasika* nature is reflected in her readiness to sacrifice herself for the sake of her husband and children in dire contrast to man who is incapable of this trait. Shyness, modesty and bashfulness are again the monopoly of the woman. Hence, the woman is on a higher plane than man. The treatment and the respectability given to women in the Sai Cult are exceedingly different from the treatment given to them in other cults.

The mode of addressing each other in Sai cult

When Vīra-Śaivism is in its zenith in the state of Karnataka, tradition informs us about the mode of address among the cultured. The younger whenever he meets the elder has to necessarily say: *oṁ! namaḥ śīvāyaḥ* (O! Lord Śiva my salutations to you). And the elder in token of his appreciation of the young man's culture will say: *namaḥ śīvaya* (You are also Śiva and my salutations are due to you).

This kind of cultural grassing could be seen easily everywhere in the Sai culture. The religious symbolism which the Sai cult has developed is very simple and the etiquettes are highly refined. Whenever two persons (male or female) meet each other in the Sai cult, they lose their identity and address each other thus:

oṁ! sāī rām, sir or *oṁ! sāī rām* or *sāī rām*

This is the *tirumantra* in the Sai cult. *Vibhūt dhāraṇā*, white dress only for men devotees, and wearing the *sārī* in a traditional way covering the neck (*grīvā*) and both the shoulders is the religious insignia and the dress prescribed to women. Every devotee of the Sai has to necessarily possess on his person either a photo or a talisman of Sai, which the devotee believes will inspire him, guide him, help him and even protect him in all walks of his life. This entrenched and deep devotion to 'Sāī Bhagavān' is strikingly visible on the face of every devotee.

Bhajana is the centrality of Sāī cult

Before we talk about the 'Sāī *bhajana*' it is necessary to look into the semantics of *bhajana* as to how it has evolved in the Indian devotional culture. The word *bhakti* (devotion) comes from the root *bhaj*. The meaning of *bhakti* is 'loyal' and 'devoted'. The root meaning of *bhaj* is 'to share in' or 'to participate in'. This root idea is never quite lost, but in classical Sanskrit it comes to mean increasingly to 'participate' in something through love and affection. In the epics we find the following meanings of *bhaj* which are incorporated in the Sai devotional culture.

1. In the *Rāmāyaṇa* we come across *bhajasva dharman* which means cultivate or enjoy *dharma*. Also it is said, let Bharata today enjoy the office of heir apparent without let or hindrance (*Rāmāyaṇa bharato bhajatam ādya yauvarajam . . .*).
2. Again in *Rāmāyaṇa* we read *bhavatan putram ekam to sulam etad bhajisyate*. Here it means 'belong to'.
3. In *Mahābhārata* it reads: *kṣamā mam bhajate*. It means 'inhere in', 'attend on' and so on.

To sum up, *bhaj* and *bhakti* mean (1) inhere in, (2) attend on, (3) belong to (4) cultivate, (5) enjoy, (6) to be loyal, and (7) to be devoted. The purpose of this analysis is only to show that the *bhajana* poetry and *bhajana* songs that are composed and sung reverberate the meaning contained in the above use of the words *bhaj*, *bhakti* and *bhajana*.

Moralisation through education

Sri Satya Sai Philosophy of Education has a profound positive content based on spiritual heritage of India and national goals that are set out by the Indian Parliament, universal perceptions and cultural perspectives. Sai Baba's philosophy of education derives from his general philosophy of life as a whole. Its watchwords are *satya*, *dharma*, *śānti* and *prema* (love) in studies and work. These four pillars of Baba's philosophy yield the four ideals of higher education: *satya* yields knowledge, *dharma* yields skill, *śānti* yields peace, stability and progress and *prema* yields balance, insight and right vision.

The Sai system of education creates in students a sense of purity (*pavitratā*) of thought, word and deed and above all it makes them better human beings who can build a new India brimming with morality and dignity of labour. We see here a harmonious blend of secular education and religious education. A computer science student is expected to chant the *puruṣa-sūkta*, *mantra-puṣpa*, *rudra-namakam* and *camakam* along with their meaning. There is a blending of science and spirituality. All kinds of 'excellences' bloom here. The educational system is a blending of all the religions of India. All *dharma*s take their nourishment here. The habits, the character, the traits and the total personality of the students here will be a perfect figure soon after they complete their studies. They become the true bearers of Sai culture in the future society. All education from kinder-garten to a doctoral degree is totally free: boarding, lodging, travel and medical — everything is free. The students are selected through an All-India entrance examination and then in a personal interview by Sai Baba. (*Vide*, Dr. K. Hanumanthappa, Vice-Chancellor's article in the *Proceedings of the Symposium on Higher Education*, 1993).

Water programme

Āpo vai brahma — says the *Taittirīya Upaniṣad*. In consonance with the motto of service to the needy, Sai Baba has launched a programme for providing water to one million people. The Sai-water-scheme with a cost of Rs. 500 crore was taken up and completed on 23 November 1995, and inaugurated by the Prime Minister of India.

Super speciality hospital

In consonance with the famous saying *vaidyo nārāyaṇo hariḥ* (the Doctor is Nārāyaṇa), Sai Baba has constructed a super-speciality hospital at a cost of Rs. 500 crore. In this hospital operations relating to transplantation of heart and kidneys are conducted free of cost and health-care is provided to thousands of people.

Bhajana mandira

The *mandira* was constructed in accordance with the glorious descriptions of *vaikuṇṭha* as it is found in the *Viṣṇu Purāṇa* and the *Bhāgavata Purāṇa*. As we enter the Prasantinilayam, we see the *navagraha-maṇḍapa*, the Lord Gaṇeśa, the Maheśvara, the Lord Hanumān, the Buddha, the Jesus Christ and all that which represents a kind of religious tolerance and religious co-existence. *Sva-mata dharma ācaraṇa* and *para-mata dharma sahanatā* with love are the key *mantra*s of the Sai culture.

17

Mother Teresa: The Mission of Love

P.J. Titus

MOTHER Teresa was born in an Albanian family on the 26th of August 1910 as the last of three children in a devoted Catholic family. They were a very happy family. Her mother used to serve food to the poor in the neighbourhood. When Agnes (her Christened name) was 9 years old, her father died. She learned how to face poverty and hardship with her mother who worked hard to support the family.

Agnes

At the age of 18, Agnes decided to become a missionary in India. In order to do that, she became a nun. She joined in the 'Order of the Sisters of Loreto'. On 1st December 1928, two nuns left on a voyage to India. It was on 6 the January 1929 that, they arrived in Kolkata. On 23rd May 1929, she changed her name to Teresa. Teresa was sent to Darjeeling for training. She was to teach at the Loreto Convent School there. Subsequently Teresa took her final vows in 1937 and she was appointed Principal of St. Mary's School at Entally, Kolkata. She used to go out and see the poor on the streets. She taught poor children in a Bengali language school. She became a teacher there.

In 1943, there was a famine in Bengal. Five million people died and many fled to Calcutta. The streets of Calcutta were full of starving and dying people and the Loreto School became a refugee centre. Teresa became a Mother and began to care for the poor, abandoned children. Hundreds came to be cared for.

Nobody knows how many poor were in Kolkata. Millions kept on coming and also dying, and Mother Teresa went on serving. In 1946, Hindu-Muslim violence started and thousands of people were killed. The sisters and the girls helped the victims of violence. Teresa experienced the famine and the effects of hatred. These events in the history of India made young Teresa to serve the poor by coming out of the convent walls.

Teresa: The Embodiment of love

On 12th April 1948, her superiors released her from the convent to work on the streets among the poor. In December 1948, Teresa opened her first school as her first project. People began to send her gifts to furnish the school and home with basic necessities. She went to medical sisters in the city of Patna to learn how to nurse the poor. In 1948 Mother Teresa started her work in Kolkata among those who were at the very bottom of human society — the destitute, the outcastes, the mentally handicapped, the homeless sleeping on the streets, those dying on the streets without anybody to claim the body but the trash dumpsters. She used to collect the leftover from homes to feed the hungry. She started with no money at all. She had deep faith in Jesus to provide for all her needs.

Teresa took a cheap white cotton *sārī* like the poor Bengālī women wore and identified herself with the poor. The sisters always took the worst dirty jobs, cleaning up the dying and burying the dead. They gave the poor destitute 'death with dignity'. During her early days in Kolkata, Kālī temple priests and a few Hindus objected to her presence because she was, a Christian and they feared that she would convert the destitute to her religion. But she did not. Once a priest got sick with TB so that no hospital would receive him but Mother Teresa did. A Muslim gave her the first proper house to train sisters and help the needy. God did not divide man into Hindu-Muslim-Christian but man did. From the very beginning of her work in Kolkata, Teresa tried to help those who were dying, abandoned on the streets of Kolkata. The sisters began feeding the hungry children. The numbers grew rapidly. Her task was almost impossible, as over three million people in Kolkata were homeless. Mother Teresa said:

> My life is devoted to Christ. . . . It is for him that I breathe and see. I can't bear the pain when people call me a social worker. Had I been in social work, I would have left it long ago. (p. 26)

Today 'The Missionaries of Charity' have more than 140 schools in India alone. 'The Missionaries of Charity' take a vow of absolute poverty, and most of their possessions are held in common. No sister is allowed to receive personal gifts and she is allowed to read only religious books. To become a sister of charity, one has to have a deep desire for God and humanity and a constructive nine years of practical training. Mother Teresa said,

> No one is indispensable. God has many means and ways. All our work should be out of love. (p. 33)

The 'Missionaries of Charity' feed six thousand people everyday in the worst slum areas of the world. The French journalist, Sandro Bordignon writes in '*She cares*' as follows:

> I believe no other philosopher or humanist has such a lively sense of humanity and the value of every human being. (p. 34)

Mother Teresa said, "Give until it hurts". Sandro Bordignon writes that the Mother used to start her day at 4.30 a.m. loving, caring and feeding the needy. Over and over again the Mother repeated the fundamental message, ". . . Serve Jesus in the distressing disguise of the poor". (p. 35) Mother Teresa said, "What can you do? Help one needy person on the street, at home, in the neighbourhood. Help one, begin with the poorest of the poor". The Mother said, "Touch a leper with your compassion". 670 mobile clinics of Missionaries of Charity were serving six million people a year. By 1988, there were over 3000 sisters and novices and also 7000 co-workers (not nuns) to help. There were 300 houses in the world, more than half of them outside India.

Once Mother Teresa replied,

> Today talking about the poor is fashion. Knowing, loving and serving the poor is quite a different matter. (p. 41)

Charlotte Gray remarks on her sacrifice and dedication, "One woman, one world, one heart".

Missionaries of Charity

Mother Teresa helped millions of the world's poorest people and her fame gradually spread. She had received honorary degrees, the John F. Kennedy Award in 1972 and the Nobel Peace Prize in 1979. It was in December 1979, that Mother Teresa went to Norway to receive the highest award — The Nobel Peace Prize. Then Mother Teresa said, "Personally I am unworthy. I accept it gratefully in the Name of the poor". The money was spent to feed the starving poor and to build homes for the homeless (p. 5). India recognised her as a symbol of charity. The former President of India, N. Sanjeeva Reddy, presenting the title *Bharata Ratna* to Mother Teresa, said:

> She embodies in herself compassion and love of humanity as few in history have done. Her entire life has been a personification of service and compassion. They are the imperatives of human existence which are generally affirmed in words but denied in actions.

Mother Teresa was a perfect symbol of the embodiment of all divine human values, virtues, qualities and characters, and attributes of the Absolute in a living woman saint. She was a philosopher interpreting the values with her life of simplicity, sacrifice and service to humanity in the spirit of Jesus Christ. She was a practical interpreter of the values cherished by ethical philosophers with a concern for man on the streets. Mother Teresa was a practising philosopher and a living saint who stood for reality and truth. One can see the *mahīmā* of the divine love on her smiling face. Mother Teresa is the *viśuddhātmā* and worked for the *mokṣa* of the destitutes of the world — loving the unlovable, serving the undesirable, providing dignity to the destitutes of the world. Mother Teresa was a symbol of God's image in human life, the crown of the creation.

Today at a time when the number of men and women entering religious orders has declined, 'The Missionaries of Charity', the order founded by Mother Teresa, is expanding rapidly and is now working in over 70 countries. The sisters work with the poor garbage-pickers in every city slum of the nations. It is not only the story of an impressive religious phenomenon, but also one of the greatest humanitarian achievements of our time.

Reference

All the quotations cited in the paper are from Charlotte Gray, *Mother Teresa*, 1994.

18

Saints: A Biblical Perspective

P.J. Titus

THE *Webster's Dictionary* defines a 'saint' as —

> a holy person, a person who is unusually charitable, patient; but in certain churches, a person officially recognised and venerated for having attained heaven after an exceptionally holy life. (p. 422)

As per the Ecclesiastical definition, a saint is

> One who is recognised or acknowledged as having achieved sanctification, especially one who is canonised as saint by a Roman Catholic Church. One extraordinary charitable, Self-denying, set apart, consecrated for the holy office. One who is totally dedicated to God and service of humanity. A believer who is separated from the wordly pleasures and evil ways to serve Holy God.
>
> — Donald Att Water, *The Penguin Dictionary of Saints*, pp. 1-2

Sainthood

As per the *New Testament* —

> Every Christian is a saint. The concept can be much fruitful and profitable preaching and teaching. No Christian can deny his vocation to a life of holiness, who are also faithful in Jesus Christ.
>
> — Nolan B. Harmon, *The Interpreter's Bible*, vol. 4, 1953, p. 612

The Christian sainthood has an eternal perspective — that living in the present with an eternal future — and could be analysed as follows:

1. Sainthood is a divine imperative. It is the character-nature of God. The love of God includes every human being (John 3:16).
2. Sainthood is a human imperative. The condition of man has to be achieved as he has lost himself in sin. "All have sinned". (Romans 3:23)
3. Sainthood is a Christological imperative. There is only one saviour, the Lord for all nations and only one name (Acts 4:12; Mathew 1:21).
4. Sainthood is a charismatic imperative, empowered to attain sainthood (Acts 1:8).
5. Sainthood is a great commission. The imperative that inspires us to "go and make disciples". (Matthew 23: 18-20)
6. Sainthood is a call. — Every person is called to be sent and to preach the good news, the love of the Saviour (John 17:18).
7. Sainthood is an eschatological imperative. The saint lives in the hope of the coming 'Kingdom of God' at the coming of Christ (1 Thess. 4:13).

Therefore Christ is the model, *our model of sainthood.* The word 'IN CHRIST' occurs 164 times in the *New Testament* which is key to Pauline theology. The hope of Christ calling, the inheritance and the immeasurable greatness of His power working in those who believe are the key to sainthood according to the *New Testament*. The Christians have hope in the glory of inheritance in the saints of God, in the age to come through eternity. What is the best strategy for sainthood? It is nothing but to become Christ; a Christian is one who invites Christ to live in — 'Christ-in'. People may be followers of Jesus Christ and become saints. Every person can become what Christ became. Jesus Christ is the model for sainthood. In the *Bible* the word 'He became' indicates the process of Self-crucifixion (Philippians 2:1; Galatians 2:20), implying sacrifice, service and dying for the cause and people. The best strategy for sainthood is the strategy of Christ as seen in the *Bible* (Philippines 2:1-10).

1. Incarnational strategy — God became man, Christ.
2. Identification strategy — God became like us.
3. Simplification strategy — God lived among men.
4. Sacrificial strategy — Christ died on the cross for the people.
5. Obedience strategy — Christ became obedient to God.
6. Servant-leadership strategy — Christ became a servant to his disciples.
7. Suffering strategy — Christ became a suffering servant for the people.

Biblically, sainthood is synonymous with sanctification, a divine importation of the nature of God in the life of every believer. The motivating force in Christian sainthood is the Spirit of Christ's compassion, the love of God poured into the believer's heart by the Holy Spirit. This *agape*, love of God enables a person to perfection. This love is the gateway for man to enter into the arena of faith to know God. Christian sainthood is based on a personal relationship between God and man — the communion, the communication and the fellowship of God and man. A vertical and horizontal reconciliation in Christ enables a sinner to establish this divine-human relationship. This highest knowledge of God is revealed in 'His Holy Word', the *Bible* and it is placed in the community of saints. The community of faith may be filled in all the wisdom and the fullness of God into maturity (Eph. 4:11-13).

Saint and the World

God has appointed fivefold officers — Apostles, Prophets, Pastors, Teachers, Evangelists — to prepare the saints for the work of ministry in the spirit and unity of faith (Eph. 4:11-13). In this process of sainthood sanctification, unification and glorification are the three pillars of a saintly life, holy (whole) dedication to God's service. Prayer, meditation, worship, music and art of communion are the means of grace to become a living saint. The *Bible* says that people could be made righteous in Christ (I Cor. 1:30). Christ is our redemption, justification, sanctification, righteousness and we are complete in Him (I Cor. 1:30). At the second coming of Christ, the church (saints) will reach its glorification and perfection. The Resurrection of Christ is the guarantee for such a hope of the saints (I Thes. 4:13).

Obviously these canonised saints are not the only saints in the colloquial sense of the word. Countless saints are uncanonised, but known to neighbours, friends and God alone. We call them the unstring heroes of faith. Christian faithfulness and heroic actions and integrity make a life a holy life. The keyword that distinguishes the saints (sainthood) is 'heroism'. A charitable, compassionate, selfless service, holding back nothing for himself/herself but using every gift for common good, looks on oneself as every man's debtor to both friend and foe (Rom. 1:14-16). By grace, by living in Christ, one is made saint or become 'Christ-like' in life and character. Simplicity, humility, sacrifice, obedience to the will of God, crucifixion (death) for others (Gal. 2:22) is a part of the saint's lifestyle.

A believer's union with Christ, devotional disciplines, dedication to His service is a sign of sainthood. Love of God makes saints perfect in Christ and every grace will make them perfect persons in heaven when grace shall be turned into glory. It is the Will of God with sanctification (I Thes. 4:3). If any man is in Christ, he will be a new creation. He is recreated into the image and likeness of God into the original state of man in paradise (2 Cor. 5:17). Renunciation of the world-self (pride) and lust of the flesh by living 'active holiness' or maintaining social holiness leads to sainthood. God demands of us to live holy (Math. 5:38; Rom. 6:19).

In the *New Testament* (Colossians 1:2) the word, 'saint' is applied generally to the members of the Christian community. But in ecclesiastical usage, from very early times, the word 'saint' has been applied to those who have been virtuous to a heroic degree. Saints are traditionally distributed into several classes: apostles, evangelists, martyrs, confessors, originally those who had undergone imprisonment without the final crown of martyrdom and later male saints in general who were eminent for sanctity; doctors, eminent men of sacred learning; virgins, matrons and widows.

Veneration of Saints

Canonisation is the method by which the title of 'saint' has been conferred in early periods and in modern times. By the fourth century AD, the practice of venerating the saints was widespread. During the Middle Ages, however, much superstition surrounded the practice. Even before the Reformation, the Bogomils and Waldenses objected to the veneration of saints; at the time of the Reformation, the practice was generally rejected as scripturally unfounded. The Roman Catholic Council of Trent (1545-63) affirmed that it is a good and useful thing to invoke the saints on account of the benefits to be obtained from God through their intercession. The belief and practice of the Orthodox church is basically the same as that of the Roman Catholic.

Of the many saints, almost all record has perished except their names. The fullest list is found in the general table in the sixty-first volume of the *Colossal Acta Sanctorum of the Bollandists*, which mentions about 20,000 saints. The catalogue that possesses the highest ecclesiastical authority is that of the *Martyrologium Romanum*. The martyrology numbers some 2700 saints, including about 20 saints of the *Old Testament*, arranged according to the days of their celebration. Many of these saints were honoured annually with a special feast day; at one time their feast days filled about two-thirds of the Roman Catholic Church's liturgical calendar, although some of the saints had become little more than names. In 1964 Vatican Council II concluded that only saints 'of truly universal significance should be extended to the universal Church' and the others 'should be left to be celebrated by a particular church or nation or religious community'. Accordingly, in 1969, Pope Paul VI approved a reordering of the liturgical calendar to achieve the council's wish. In the revised calendar, which took effect on 1 January 1970, only 58 regular or obligatory and 92 optional feast days of saints were retained in addition to those of Christ, the Virgin Mary, saint Joseph, and the apostles.

In Christian art, representations of the saints as well as of Christ are often marked by a halo (also known as a nimbus, aureole, or glory), a ring or aura of radiance above the head or entire figure. And many of the saints are pictured with emblems by which they could readily be recognised. A martyr who had a special interest in a place was called its patron as early as the fourth century. Trades and professions had their patrons and for every disease a saint could be invoked to cure it. Among the widely known patron saints are Andrew of Scotland, Denis of France, George of England, Nicholas of Russia, Patrick of Ireland, James the Great of Spain, and Stephen of Hungary. The term hagiology or hagiography is used to denote the branch of literature that is concerned with the lives and legends of the saints.

The Process of Canonisation

Canonisation, in the Roman Catholic Church, is an act by which the Pope publicly proclaims the sanctity of a deceased person as 'saint', whom he thereupon proposes for the veneration of the universal church. Canonisation is usually the final act of a lengthy process that begins with beautification. The decree of beautification is an official declaration that a person lived a holy life and can be venerated as one of the 'blessed'. Canonisation awards the full title of 'saint'. In the Orthodox Church, the process of Canonisation is less formal and is carried out by local synods of bishops. The modern custom of Canonisation originated in the early Christian practice of paying public honour to the martyrs. For many centuries thereafter the title of 'saint' was bestowed by popular acclamation. Not until a comparatively late period was procedure equivalent to Canonisation adopted. The earliest acknowledged instance of a solemn decree of Canonisation is that of Udalric or Ulric, bishop of Augsburg, declared a saint by Pope John XV in 993. Pope Alexander III in 1171 reserved the right of canonising exclusively for the papacy. Pope Urban VIII, in two constitutions promulgated in 1625 and 1634, made more stringent regulations and laid down the Canonisation procedure that, with slight modifications, is still followed.

Canonisation, without a special dispensation, cannot be declared until 50 years have elapsed since the claimant's death. The process that precedes the decree of Canonisation seeks to establish two characteristics of the claimant according to the testimony of competent witnesses: eminent virtues, technically referred to as virtues in a 'heroic degree', and the performance of at least two authentic miracles. If the initial investigation is satisfactory, the Pope takes the cause into his own hands and issues letters assigning the cause to a committee of the Congregation for the Causes of Saints, which then examines the virtues and miracles specifically. Then the claimant's cause is said to be 'introduced'; the introduction of the cause, that is, of the pontifical process, entitles the beatification or candidate for beatification, to be called 'venerable'. Many candidates have reached this stage in the proceedings and have failed to go beyond it. If the candidate passes successfully through the proceedings, a decree of beatification is pronounced.

Beatification, since the twelfth century, means an official papal declaration that a deceased person lived a holy life and is worthy of veneration. The beatified person receives the title 'blessed'. The process leading to beatification involves an intensive examination of the life, writings and reputation of the person under consideration. It is generally a step towards Canonisation. Before the twelfth century, local bishops instituted the process and issued the declaration of beatification for their own dioceses.

Before the further process of canonisation can be instituted, witnesses must testify that the candidate has worked a certain number of miracles since beatification. The case then once more passes through the hands of several congregations, the last of which is held in the presence of the Pope when the final decree is agreed upon. The ceremony of canonisation occurs in Saint Peter's Basilica in the Vatican and is one of the most solemn and imposing of all papal functions. Equipollent or equivalent canonisation is founded upon proof of immemorial veneration, or of some papal sanction given to veneration, prior to the date of Urban VIIIs constitution. In such cases the Pope may at once pronounce the decree of Canonisation. Equipollent beatification is a summary process of a similar kind. The Pope accepts the results of the preliminary process and at once decrees beatification.

Christian Theology and Saints

C.S. Lewis says, "I believe in Christianity as I believe that the sun has risen not only because I can see it, but because by it I see everything else". Theology is meant for God-words, God-study and God-thought. J.I. Pacter says, "Theology is that science of living blessedly forever". Therefore the question arises, how to make God a living reality in everyday life? Theology is for achieving God's glory (honour and praise) and godliness is the true humanness through every life-activity. The only theology to be applied to daily life is to be a true Christian. One reason is that the movement of the *Bible* is always from the indicative to imperative, from doctrine to duty, from kerugma to dideche, from theology to ethics, from revealed truth to full extraordinary living. I would not want to be a professor of unapplied theology.

An orthodentist is a person who makes straight teeth. An orthodox (ortho = straight, doxa = glory) doctrine that lines itself with scripture is designated to be a blessing to everyday life. Theological education for all people of God is the life-long, life-based, life-oriented process of forming and transforming persons, communities into Christian maturity for the purpose of serving God and God's kingdom in the world. The whole of our life has the glorious prospect of being lived out for the great doctrines of the Christian faith. There is a difference between theologians' talking about God and living for God. In the *Bible*, Job's friends delivered lectures about God but he talked to God. Job's theology is orthodox. He spoke well of God but his wife had a negative theology.

God can never be contained by human mind. We do not control Him by theological orders, but He controls our minds and destiny. Theology begins with contemplation and admiration and not with problems. A doxological theology, truthful living for God's glory, is a proper theology of living; the doctrine that does not lead to doxology is demonic (James 2:19). The goal of Biblical theological education is to increase our love for God to make us more human. The purpose of the church and a life based on education is that the 'saints' will live for the praise of God's glory (Eph. 1:12-14), that is to live doxologically. Biblical theology should bless everyday life. We need to develop a theology of good works, a straight practice. How can people be saved by God's grace? Evangelical theology says that we are saved by grace and not by works, but faith without work is dead. The Christian task is humanising theological living. We have been dichotomising theology and practising 'theological academy' today. In the *New Testament*, in the theological community of faith every person is a theologian with application. Obedient action is the organ for further revelation. 'Do this' is Jesus concerned to His church (John 2:5, 2 Cor. 11:26). We know more through doing than knowing.

Moses who wrote the first five historic books was considered a *nabī*, a prophet without equal (Deut. 34:10). Samuel was a great prophet of Israel (2 Sam. 12). Elijah and Elisha both were prophets of fire (I Kig. 18-19). John the Baptist, a contemporary of Jesus Christ, was a great prophet in the *New Testament*. Prophecies were classified into three categories: (1) Prophecies related to the internal destiny of Israel. (2) Messianic prophesies (Isaiah 7:14, 9:6). (3) Eschatological prophesies.

Prophesis are twofold fulfilment: (1) immediate fulfilment, and (2) futuristic fulfilment. Prophets were second in command, next to Apostles in the *New Testament* (Eph. 4: 11-13). Apostles and prophets are the foundation of the church (Eph. 2:20). They were saturated with the scriptures. They were men of the spirit with power to action. The living 'saint' can be a prophet (*nabī*) who is inspired by the Holy Spirit of God and speaks exactly what he receives. The mode of inspiration is verbal. God said to Moses, "I will raise them up a prophet from among their brethren like unto thee and will put my words (verbal) in his mouth". (Due 18:18) Similarly God said to Jeremiah, "I have put my words in thy mouth" (Jeremiah 1:9) It is the miracle of the theopneustia (2 Tim 3:16) to communicate his thoughts to men. God uses men of different cultures, characters and statuses in order that his word might be accessible to all men. Inspiration safeguards individuality.

There are 17 prophets in the *Old Testament* Prophetical movement — five major prophets and 12 minor prophets. Isaiah, Jeremiah, Ezekiel, Daniel and Apocalyptic are major prophetic books. Prophetic spirit revealed the nature of God; and the Holy Spirit made revelation possible. Prophets were considered men of authority and were held high in society as social reformers and social advocates for socio-economic justice. A prophet is a champion of righteousness and justice. Those who receive Christ are rooted in His love and are preserved and sanctified. Christians are beings made perfect and are becoming people. (John 1:12) "As many as have received Him, to them He gave power (authority, right) to become children of God". We are being transformed from faith to faith, from glory to glory relocating the image of Christ in us (2 Cor. 3:18).

Some of the Christian saints in the church of India were Sadhu Sunder Singh, Pundit Rama Bhai (Mukti Mission) and Mother Teresa. In the History of the *Bible*, we have St. Joseph, St. Mary, St. Mathew, St. Mark, St. Luke, St. John, St. Peter, St. Paul and others. Time and Space do not permit me to write their biographical accounts. The Christian saints were all social reformers, champions of righteousness, social justice and spiritual giants in a world. A true saint's work is for national unity, integration, peace, justice and freedom of all people of God. 'Thus saith the Lord' is their address and 'Let my people go' is their socio-political slogan. They are leaders for social redemption. Man is neither totally good nor totally bad but man is totally redeemable, alive and saintly; and can reach a higher excellence in the knowledge of Christ.

From the very beginning Christianity has been an ethical religion. Its ethics are rooted and grounded in its faith and worship. No one can read the Sermon on the Mount without realising the very high moral standards, with respect both to inner motive and outward conduct, as set forth by Jesus Christ to his disciples. Even Mahatma Gandhi and Martin Luther King were motivated by the non-violence and high moral teachings of Jesus. There must be a peace in the life of the community of saints for spiritual discipline. There are strong ethical implications of the Christian faith in daily life. Those who call themselves by the name of Christ shall mean something distinctive by it: 'these people are followers of Christ'. They are distinguished by their righteous lifestyle. The kingdom of God is only for the righteous.

Sainthood and Spirituality

Sainthood is not an isolated state of mind but it is spirituality expressed in our daily life's activities. It is a level of being and doing. Active life has to be linked with the spiritual resource within. Sainthood is not a part-time activity; it has to be integrated into every movement of our lives. Sainthood and spirituality are uncharted territory. Each one has to walk one's own path of faith. Be creative, vigilant of what you are, the way you think, feel and act. Sainthood is living in the presence of the eternal one. To be open to the love of God and to share sainthood is the care of human value, way of living and divine being.

Jesus Christ is the greatest philosopher who has ever lived in human history, who interpreted the Holy Scriptures with a new covenantal perspective and His followers called His documents the *New Testament* in the Holy *Bible*. He Himself was a student of *Old Testament* Scriptures and He interpreted the Law with grace and glory (John 1:1, 14). Jesus Christ is the final unique and ultimate revelation of the personal true living God. God of the *Bible* is a person and a personal God. The word that, it does not apply to Biblical perspective of Godhead. He is the Supreme Being, Supreme mind, and Supreme intelligence, who is the creator of all existence. He exists eternally beyond the creation. From eternity to eternity God is. His Name is 'I AM THAT I AM'. He who that comes to God must believe that God is (Heb. 11:6) and a new order of them diligently seek Him. He is the Alpha and the Omega. He transcends all creation. He manifested Himself in creation (Psalms 19:1), in history, in logos (Reason) faith, experience, in His word and by His Holy Spirit. These are the epistemological tools to know the God of the *Bible*. Faith is foundation. We know by faith (Heb. 11:1). Faith comes by hearing and hearing by the word of God (Rom. 10:8-17). The Holy Scriptures are written that we may know Him and have eternal life (John 5:20). When *guru*s of the Vedas sought after truth, Jesus declared, "I am the Truth". When seekers prayed to show the way, Jesus said, "I am the way", When the seekers sought for light in darkness, He said, "I am the Light" (John 14:6) "I am the way, the truth and the life". Truth is a person. God is absolute truth. God is love, light and life.

The personal nature of the absolute truth is made known by His revelation, proclamation and teachings. In Christ man can know God. He is the expressed image of God (Heb. 1:1). Man can see the face of God in the face of Jesus Christ. Through Jesus Christ the knowability of God, the visibility of God, the believability of God, the possibility of knowing God, the authenticity of living faith experience is now a positive motivation for us all (Math 5). In India, philosophers and interpreters of Vedānta must contribute to the positive thinking, creative thinking and indigenous thinking in place of negativism, passivism, pessimism and fatalism, that have destructive influence on the new generation. Spirituality, morality and civility must be cultivated in the hearts through scriptural interpretation.

The visibility of God is made possible by the incarnation of God in Jesus Christ (Phil 2:1). He incarnated, identified with humanity, simplified Himself that man can know God. He humbled Himself, the highest quality of God. He was obedient to the sovereign will of His Heavenly Father. He suffered for the sin of man, was crucified and resurrected for our justification. By resurrection with the fallible, irrefutable, convincing evidence, He was declared Son of God (Rom 1:4). He became servant of all (John 13) by washing the feet of fellowmen. He suffered with the suffering humanity. His atonement is the only historical sacrifice for the sins of humanity. Jesus died for man's sin. A believer is dead to sin. A sinner dies in sin. Sin is not an illusion/*māyā*/ vanity, but it is a reality. Somebody said, "Humanity minus vanity equals divinity". A sinless person is a 'living saint'. Jesus was sinless, perfect God-man and He is the embodiment of Theo-anthropo. His philosophy is non-violence. He had no military and no army to defend His kingdom. He loved His enemies and prayed for their forgiveness. He said, "I give you peace", peace that passeth all understanding. He is the Prince of Peace. He is wonderful Counsellor (Isaiah 9:6). He is the suffering Messiah of the prophetic books. He is the wounded healer. He is the great physician. By believing in Him, one can experience the New Life in Him. One who receives Him, believes in Him becomes the saint of God (John 1:12). We are now being transformed into His image (2 Cori. 3:18). Man was created in the image of God in His likeness — now in Christ that original image in paradise is regained by Christ (I Cori. 5:17).

If any man is in Christ he is a new creation/humanity. Life is changed. Evil men are converted and transformed by the power of His Holy Name. By calling on the Name of Jesus, sinners find pardon and cleansing. Demons are cast out in His Name. Sick are healed by His Name. You can identify God with that sweet Name. He is our Saviour, Salvation. He is Emmanuel — God with us. We can experience His unconditioned love and forgiveness by total surrender to Him. We can win victory through surrender to His divine will, divine word and Holy Spirit. We are destined to win. He was born to be crucified to set us free from all bondages of sin, vanities and corruptions of carnality. We must maintain a personal relationship with God through reconciliation (2 Cor. 5:18-20). Through reconciliation we shall become like Him (I John 3:1). Man must find His unity in God (John 17:17-21). God is love. The goal of a follower of Jesus is to become like the Master. He is truly a 'saint'.

The Contributors

V. Badarayana Murthy, Purana Vijanana Mandira, 151-12, Devanathachar Street, Chamarajpet, Bangalore-18.

B.V.S. Bhanusree, Assistant Professor, Department of Philosophy, Andhra University, Waltair, Vishakhapatnam-530 003.

P. George Victor, Professor, Department of Philosophy, Andhra University, Waltair, Vishakhapatnam-530 003.

V. Gopalakrishnaiah, Rtd. Professor, Andhra University, Waltair, Vishakhapatnam-530 003.

M. Gopalakrishna Reddy, Former Vice-Chancellor, Andhra University, Waltair, Vishakhapatnam-530 003.

S.D.A. Joga Rao, Associate Professor, Department of Philosophy, Andhra University, Waltair, Vishakhapatnam-530 003.

Monika Talapatra, (Head, Department of Philosophy, Serampore College) D.A. 182 Salt Lake, Kolkata-700 064.

Nimita Kar and Bijayananda, Kar, Rtd. Professor of Philosophy, Utkal University, Bhubaneswar.

T. Padma, Rtd. Professor, Department of English, Andhra University, Waltair, Vishakhapatnam-530 003.

K.R. Rajani, Assistant Professor, Department of Philosophy, Andhra University, Waltair, Vishakhapatnam-530 003.

G.S.R. Raju, Rtd. Profesor, Department of Philosophy, D.N.R. College, Bhimavaram.

S. Satyanarayana, Professor, Department of Philosophy, Andhra University, Waltair, Vishakhapatnam-530 003.

V.N. Seshagiri Rao, Department of Philosophy, Mysore University, Manasa Gangotri, Mysore-570 006.

B.P. Siddhashrama, Professor of Philosophy, Karnatak University, Dharwad.

S.C. Suguna Kumari, Assistant Professor, Department of Philosophy, Andhra University, Waltair, Vishakhapatnam-530 003.

G. Sundara Ramaiah, Rtd. Professor, Department of Philosophy, Andhra University, Waltair, Vishakhapatnam-530 003.

P.J. Titus, Founder/President C.O.T.R., College of Ministries, Dorathota, Box 3, Bhimunipatnam-531 163.

Index